THE
OHIO
LITERARY TRAIL

A Guide

BETTY WEIBEL

THE
History
PRESS

*Happy travels!
Betty Weibel*

Published by The History Press
Charleston, SC
www.historypress.com

Copyright © 2021 by Betty Weibel
All rights reserved

Cover images: Portrait of Toni Morrison courtesy of the photographer, ©2015 Timothy Greenfield-Sanders. Malabar Farm Big House photo by Lindsey Burnett. James Thurber typewriter photo courtesy of Thurber House. Ohioana Literary Trail banner designed by Kathryn Powers, Ohioana Library Association.

First published 2021

Manufactured in the United States

ISBN 9781467149341

Library of Congress Control Number: 2021931245

CONTENTS

CONTENTS

CONTENTS

The Ohio Literary Trail

Presented by Ohioana Library Association

The Ohio Literary Trail shines a spotlight on Ohio's role in shaping culture and literature worldwide. Visitors will discover the state's rich literary landscape through landmark destinations, historical markers that recognize literary achievements, and book festivals dedicated to readers and writers.

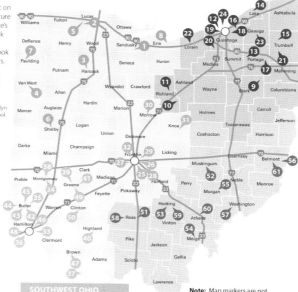

Note: Map markers are not exact locations.

NORTHWEST OHIO

1. Clyde Historical Museum and Sherwood Anderson historical marker
2. Toledo-Lucas County Public Library - Carolyn Keene Exhibit and Toledo's First High School and Toledo Lucas County Public Library
3. The Mazza Museum
4. The Brumback Library historical marker
5. House of Four Pillars historical marker
6. Lois Lenski historical marker
7. Paulding County Carnegie Library h. m.*
8. Sandusky Library historical marker

Book Festival: Claire's Day

NORTHEAST OHIO

9. Haines House
10. Malabar Farm and Louis Bromfield h. m.*
11. Oak Hill Cottage
12. Ohio Center for the Book /Cleveland Public Library
13. Wick Poetry Center and Reinberger Children's Library Center
14. Daniel Carter Beard historical marker
15. Bristol Public Library historical marker
16. Cleveland Hts. Library - Harvey Pekar
17. Hart Crane historical marker
18. East Cleveland Public Library h. m.*
19. James Mercer Langston Hughes h. m.*
20. The Oxcart Library historical marker h. m.*
21. Earl Derr Biggers historical marker
22. Toni Morrison Reading Room Helen Steiner Rice historical marker
23. Second H. School-Burton Library h. m.*
24. Home of Superman historical marker

Book Festival: Buckeye Book Fair

CENTRAL OHIO

25. Thurber House Museum and Thurber Center and James Thurber historical marker
26. The Billy Ireland Cartoon Library & Museum and Jerome Lawrence and Robert E. Lee Theatre Research Institute
27. Ohioana Library Association
28. Wagnalls Memorial Library
29. Columbus Metropolitan Main Library h. m.*
30. Dawn Powell historical marker
31. John Crowe Ransom and The Kenyon Review h. m.*
32. Wilbur H. Siebert Collection historical marker

Book Festival: Ohioana Book Festival

For more information visit Ohioana.org.

SOUTHWEST OHIO

33. Harriet Beecher Stowe House and Harriet Beecher Stowe historical marker
34. Paul Laurence Dunbar House and State Memorial and Paul Laurence Dunbar h. m.*
35. McGuffey House and Museum and William H. McGuffey historical marker
36. The Mercantile Library
37. The Rankin House
38. Natalie Clifford Barney historical marker
39. Hallie Quinn Brown historical marker
40. Milton Caniff historical marker
41. Virginia Hamilton historical marker
42. William Dean Howells historical marker
43. Fannie Hurst historical marker
44. McCloskey Museum
45. Percy MacKaye-"The Poet's Shack" h. m.*
46. The Jacob Rader Marcus Center of the American Jewish Archives historical marker
47. Albert Nelson Marquis/Who's Who h. m.*
48. Public Library of Cincinnati and Hamilton County historical marker
49. Helen Hooven Santmyer historical marker
50. Wilmington Library historical marker

Book Festival: Books by the Banks

SOUTHEAST OHIO

51. Dard Hunter Studios historical marker
52. Zane Grey and National Road Museum
53. Grandma Gatewood Trail
54. James Edwin Campbell historical marker Ambrose Bierce historical marker
55. Frances Dana Gage historical marker
56. William Dean Howells historical marker
57. Putnam Family Library - Belpre Farmers Library historical marker
58. Burton Egbert Stevenson historical marker
59. Tessa Sweazy Webb historical marker
60. Western Library Association - The Coonskin Library historical marker
61. James Arlington Wright historical marker

Book Festival: Spring Literary Festival

* Historical Marker is noted as "h. m."

The Ohio Literary Trail, hosted by Ohioana Library Association. *Leslie King design.*

FOREWORD

The world is a book and those who do not travel read only one page.

No one knows for sure the exact source of that quote (it's been attributed to Saint Augustine). Whoever said it, it's a wise and wonderful thought. And perfectly suited to *The Ohio Literary Trail: A Guide*, for it's all about books *and* travel!

In her preface, Betty Weibel has shared the genesis of how this book came to be: our conversation in early 2020 about the ninetieth anniversary of the first Nancy Drew mysteries by Toledo writer Mildred Wirt Benson (the original "Carolyn Keene"). As it happened, the Ohioana Library Association, just the year before, had celebrated that same milestone. Since its founding in 1929 by Ohio first lady Martha Kinney Cooper, Ohioana has been dedicated to collecting, preserving and celebrating Ohio literature. Through its collection, events and publications, Ohioana connects readers and Ohio writers and promotes the Buckeye State as one of the great literary centers of our nation.

Ohio has had a robust literary culture since its early years as a state. It continues to shape and influence literature on a global scale. Some of the world's greatest writers have called Ohio home at one time or another. They've often spoken of the state's impact on their lives and careers. Lorain's Toni Morrison won nearly every literary award imaginable, culminating in the Nobel Prize. When Morrison came to Columbus in 1988 to accept the Ohioana Career Medal, she expressed her heartfelt indebtedness to her home state: "Ohio is paramount in so much of my work. My gratitude to you and fellow Ohioans is profound—not only for the award but for the gift to my imagination."

Another writer, Pulitzer Prize winner Anthony Doerr, wrote to Betty Weibel about his Ohio roots and how they influenced him:

> *Ohio has been instrumental to everything about my life, of course, as all home places are. Growing up in Geauga County made me who I am—I learned to work hard, to pay attention to nature, to be loyal, to drive in the snow, to rake leaves, and the simple pleasure of reading a book under a tree....My dad ran a small business in Chagrin Falls for decades and taught me so much about persistence, hard work, risk-taking, relationships, kindness, humor, and how to stay loyal to the Browns. My mom taught at a Montessori school in Cleveland Heights, and then at University School in Hunting Valley, and to describe how important she has been to my writing in such a small space would be impossible. But here's a try: first and foremost, she was and is a reader....My mom, together with the local library, helped me fall in love with books.*

National Book Award winner Jacqueline Woodson was born in Columbus but moved out of state with her family when she was only one year old. Yet her tie to her birthplace remains strong: "I still say that I'm Buckeye to the Bone. Ohio was my first home. My dad, aunt, and cousins are all still there. I love that I can claim the Midwest, the South, and Brooklyn as home, and in each place, some part of me is infinitely grounded. So, yeah—even if you can't hear the twang, Ohio is a part of me."

The fact that you can visit places in our state where many of Ohio's greatest writers have lived and worked is truly special. But the trail is not only about the past. As you'll see from the guide, it also invites you to participate in wonderful literary events happening each year around the state, where you can meet the most talented authors writing today. In this way, the Ohio Literary Trail is linking Ohio's literary past, present and future.

We are grateful to Betty Weibel for bringing the idea to us and for spearheading the project from an intriguing concept to an accomplished reality. And now, with *The Ohio Literary Trail: A Guide*, she has taken it even further than we imagined. We deeply appreciate that Betty is donating her royalties from the book to Ohioana, helping us to continue promoting and celebrating Ohio literature.

The world is indeed a book. And Ohio is a world itself, with places associated with many of the fascinating authors who have made their mark here. *The Ohio Literary Trail: A Guide* is a road map that I believe will take you to some truly memorable experiences. And I hope to meet you along the way.

—DAVID E. WEAVER
Executive Director
Ohioana Library Association

PREFACE

The original idea behind creating *The Ohio Literary Trail: A Guide* came from a blend of experiences over the years: promoting Ohio for the state's Division of Travel and Tourism; working for the Ohio Bicentennial Commission when the historical literary markers had their growth spurt; serving as a board member for the Ohio History Connection; and, most recently, serving as a board member for the Ohioana Library Association.

Ohioana had been involved in collaborating on an Ohio Literary Trail map in conjunction with the Ohio Center for the Book and the State Library of Ohio. The first map was produced in 1957, with updates every decade or so, but the printed map was cumbersome in size and limited in its listings.

A conversation with Ohioana executive director David Weaver about the ninetieth anniversary of teen sleuth Nancy Drew (initially penned by Ohio author Mildred Wirt Benson) led to a deeper discussion of the depth of Ohio's literary talent, and the idea for a new, expanded, digital Ohio Literary Trail map was born; it debuted online at ohioana.org in 2020, identifying seventy-two literary destinations. Selection of the sites was based on the original literary map, historical markers with a literary theme and suggestions from the staffs of Ohioana Library Association and Ohio History Connection, in addition to author research.

As Ohio continues to produce great talent and influence the literary world, the trail map will continue to be updated with new destinations that invite discovery and inspire the next generation of writers. Worthy sites that may have missed the initial selection process will be added in the future. As host of the digital map, the Ohioana Library Association will field those suggestions for review and action. Also, 100% percent of author royalties from this book will be donated to the Ohioana Library Association. Through its work, I hope that these wonderful sites will benefit from increased awareness and visitors who will support their continued existence.

Although my name is on this guide as the author, I feel that this book is a compilation of information written by local historians and community representatives who proudly care for the literary destinations (museums, libraries and historic sites) and pursued the development and dedication of historical markers in their towns to honor the accomplishments of those who came before them. Without their efforts, the history would be forgotten. These sites should be visited. The historical markers that dot Ohio's landscapes are not there to be driven past—they are there to be read and remembered. My hope is that sharing the marker texts in this book will make it easier to keep Ohio's literary history alive.

Ohio has so much to offer, even during a pandemic when travels are limited. The Ohio Literary Trail presents many reasons to take a road trip and explore. Even if a historic site may be closed, there are numerous markers to visit and opportunities to walk in the path of literary greats to see Ohio as they did. This book is your personal invitation.

ACKNOWLEDGEMENTS

How do you write a travel guide during a pandemic when most of the sites are closed and the staff are either working from home or furloughed? Heartfelt thanks go out to the organizations participating in the Ohio Literary Trail that helped me compile the facts, photos and travel tips to encourage visitors to discover the numerous literary treasures Ohio has to offer. Information was gathered through interviews, surveys and research.

At the heart of this project is the Ohioana Library Association team, including Morgan Peters, Kathryn Powers, Courtney Brown and their leader, David Weaver. Without them, this project would never have gotten off the ground. Their wonderful publication, *Ohioana Quarterly*, which features an "Ohio Literary Landmark" series, was a frequently used source for this guide because the articles by the staff and board member Bryan Loar were filled with valuable information and photos.

Laura Russell, historical markers coordinator at the Ohio History Connection, went above and beyond to help me identify the literary-related markers from among the 1,700 Ohio history markers listed at remarkableohio.org. She also helped me research details, photos and even the mysterious disappearance of some of the markers, which I didn't realize could happen. Additionally, staff members from the Ohio History Connection played a key role, particularly in searching for numerous photos. Special thanks to Emmy Beach, Lily Birkhimer and Lisa Wood, as well as Jamison Pack, Steve George and Andy Verhoff, for their support.

Ohioana Quarterly 2016 cover featuring the Ohio Literary Trail map, a joint project of three organizations that promote Ohio writers: Ohioana Library Association, Ohio Center for the Book at Cleveland Public Library and the State Library of Ohio. *Designed by Christine Colnar at the Cleveland Public Library.*

Many historic site, museum and library representatives took time out of their schedules for interviews, numerous fact-checking questions, editing and photo research. Those key figures are listed alphabetically by their organization, and I apologize in advance if I miss thanking someone: Robb Hyde from Alliance Area Preservation Society; Julia Wiesenberg from Buckeye Book Fair; Diane Bush from Claire's Day; Gene Smith from the Clyde Museum and photographer Bianca Garza; Chris Rice from Cincinnati and Hamilton County Public Library; Alex Heckman from Dayton History; Sheryl Banks from Heights Libraries; Jennifer Black and Cheri Campbell from Lorain Public Library; Lori Morey from Malabar Farm State Park; Nancy Follmer, Celeste Swanson and Janet Sohngen from McCloskey Museum; Steve Gordon from McGuffey House and Museum; Amy Hunter from Mercantile Library; Debbie Allender from the Museum Association of East Muskingum; Don Boozer from Ohio Center for the Book; Patrick Quackenbush and Stephanie O'Grady from Ohio Department of Natural Resources; Nena Couch and Nancy Colvin from Ohio State Libraries; Michelle Baldini from Reinberger Children's Library Center;

Alan Wigton from Richland County Historical Society; Abigail Zhang from Harriet Beecher Stowe House; Leah Wharton from Thurber House; Nancy Eames from Toledo Lucas County Public Library; Natasha Lancaster from the University of Findlay's Mazza Museum; Tami Morehouse from the Wagnalls Memorial Library; Jan Vaughn from Warren-Trumbull County Public Library; and David Hassler from Wick Poetry Center.

My deepest gratitude to my talented friends Leslie King, who designed the Ohio Literary Trail map and helped me with photo conversions and selections for this book, and Flo Cunningham, who provided expert editing. Flo is a master of detail, and without her assistance and encouragement, I could never have tackled this project or finished. Writing this book was like building a jigsaw puzzle, and without their skills and support, I would still be trying to fit it all together.

At a time when the publishing industry was shut down and so many wonderful projects were on hold due to the pandemic, I knew that it was a long shot to reach out to my former publisher The History Press/Arcadia Publishing to explain the new Ohio Literary Trail and my concept to create a travel guide. I connected with acquisitions editor John Rodrigue, who not only listened but also championed my idea and helped me through a very short turnaround schedule so this could be ready by spring, when people are longing to travel and book festivals are back on the calendar.

The support of my family is key to my writing. My daughter, Claire, helped get this idea off the ground with support, editing and research advice that continued from book development to completion. My brother, Michael, an experienced Ohio road warrior, helped me understand how to get from one site to another and how to group them for this book. And finally, my husband, Dave, kept my dog and horses fed and picked up dinners when I labored over countless drafts. My deepest gratitude to all.

Harriet Beecher Stowe House, a home and museum that also hosts a historical marker that shares Stowe's story. *Courtesy of Ohio History Connection.*

National Road (Route 40), which paved the way for travel across America. The region's raw materials opened up the area for mining and drilling, and the natural beauty attracts visitors to the state parks and national forest, where a portion of the magical Appalachian Trail appeals to hikers like literary subject Grandma Gatewood, who inspired many books herself.

Chapter 2

LITERARY LANDMARKS, HISTORICAL MARKERS AND FESTIVALS

What's the Difference?

MUSEUMS, LIBRARIES AND HISTORIC HOMES ARE LANDMARK DESTINATIONS

The Ohio Literary Trail will guide your discovery of unique museums, libraries and historic sites or homes that showcase the state's rich literary history. At some sites, you may spend an hour; others can fill more than a day of exploring. To fully appreciate each literary site and heritage, take a little extra time to observe the community and surrounding environment that influenced the creative process.

Museums and historical homesites are proud centerpieces of communities that take visitors deep into the culture of Ohio. Each site is operated by local and/or state historical societies, and in some cases, they are site partners with the Ohio History Connection.

In the destination libraries on the trail, you will discover more than books to check out. They were selected because they house special literary collections, reading rooms, statues, art or even literary exhibits worth visiting.

Within these destination listings are helpful descriptions that will encourage you to explore more. Before you go, visit the websites to confirm hours, admission pricing, special events or exhibits. A preview of each region's offerings can help you decide how to map your cultural outing. You can also prepare with extra research on the communities that are home to the literary landmarks and nearby attractions.

For example, the Ohio Department of Natural Resources (ODNR) State Park Storybook Trails opened in 2019, and four more followed in 2020. In partnership with the Ohio Governor's Imagination Library and Dolly Parton's Imagination Library, ODNR launched the program to promote reading and a love of the outdoors for families and their youngest members. Each trail features a different story, and families can walk their way through some of Ohio's most picturesque trails while learning about different aspects of nature from the books and authors who were inspired by nature. All five of the trails are included in this book, with one in each of Ohio's regions; new trails will be added in the future.

Historical Markers Are Short Stops on the Trail

Ohio has about 1,700 historical markers, and this guide highlights those with a literary theme. You could spend days traversing Ohio on a literary marker scavenger hunt. Most are located outdoors in public places like parks or community pathways; there are no visitation hours or admission fees and, in some cases, no specific street address, other than a description of location, like "south end of the parking lot." The markers are visible to pedestrians, ideally on foot. However, since many people only see the markers from a car, this guide includes the complete marker text, as well as GPS coordinates should you decide not to leave your vehicle.

Very few states have such a robust historical marker program, and Ohio's is the direct result of the Ohio History Connection. Each historical marker is listed at Ohio History Connection's website (remarkableohio.org). Andy Verhoff of the Ohio History Connection explained the importance of the markers: "Some represent historic sites that remain intact, while others note places and stories that are only memories. Either way, markers are like pushpins on the map of Ohio and reveal the many layers of our state's history."

The Ohio marker program was launched in 1953 as part of Ohio's sesquicentennial celebration of statehood. Ever since the first marker, the process has remained the same. Local organizations and people around the state propose topics for markers, complete an application, raise funds and work with Ohio History Connection staff to fact-check and finalize the marker's text.

Ohio historical markers are produced by Sewah Studios in Marietta. Finishing touches to the markers are applied in the paint shop. *Courtesy of Ohio History Connection/Andy Verhoff.*

During Ohio's bicentennial (2003), a special effort was made to erect historical markers under a themed umbrella to ensure that some of the most important facets of Ohio's history were included. Targeted markers were erected in twenty-one categories, including "Literary Ohio."

The Ohio Literary Trail includes more than fifty historical markers dedicated predominantly by the Ohio History Connection and the Ohio Bicentennial Commission, and a few are from United for Libraries/ American Library Association literary landmark program. The historical markers celebrate Ohio's diversity through an eclectic range of literary greats who influenced feminism and women's rights, Black history, religion, LGBTQ+ rights and American culture through literature.

"In communities of every size, citizens supported their local marker dedication and brought attention to the history they honored," said Stephen George, former executive director of the Ohio Bicentennial Commission. "For example, in the small town of Mount Gilead, the late author Dawn Powell was honored with a marker. Many people were unaware she grew up in Mount Gilead and went on to become an admired author drawing on her life in small-town Ohio. So many small towns in Ohio produced outstanding writers who changed or shaped our country's culture. The Bicentennial's Literary Ohio-targeted markers drew attention to the Buckeye State's wide range of contributions to American literary culture."

FESTIVALS CONNECT READERS AND WRITERS

After exploring the heritage presented on the Ohio Literary Trail, turn your focus to Ohio's current writers and books. For a true literary celebration that unites readers and writers, the final part of this guide features annual book fairs and festivals from each region. First up on the calendar is the Ohioana Book Festival in Columbus. Others include Wooster's Buckeye Book Fair, Books by the Banks in Cincinnati, the Athens Spring Literary Festival and Claire's Day in Northwest Ohio. The big events feature authors, illustrators, poets and more, with fun activities for everyone.

Whether you attend one or all of the book festivals, you will have an opportunity to connect with writers who may one day be immortalized on the Ohio Literary Trail.

Readers interact with writers at the Ohioana Book Festival. *Photo by Mary Rathke.*

PART II

Northwest Ohio

Northwest Ohio region on the Ohio Literary Trail map. *Leslie King design.*

Chapter 3

LUCAS COUNTY

Nancy Drew Collection/Toledo Lucas County Public Library

Toledo, Ohio

(Ohio Literary Trail Map no. 2)

Location: 325 North Michigan Street, Toledo, OH 43604; check hours at toledolibrary.org

Honors the fictitious teen sleuth Nancy Drew, first penned by Toledo writer Mildred Wirt, ghostwriting under the name Carolyn Keene.

Nancy Drew made her debut in 1930 in *The Secret of the Old Clock*. The author, Carolyn Keene, was actually a pseudonym for Mildred "Millie" Wirt (1905–2002), a young Iowa-born writer hired by publisher Edward Stratemeyer. Although the idea for the series was the publisher's, it was Wirt who developed the sixteen-year-old character and brought her to life, writing twenty-three of the popular mystery novels. The last one Wirt wrote, *The Clue of the Velvet Mask*, came out in 1953, when she was living in Toledo. Wirt was a columnist for the *Toledo Blade* for more than fifty years, until she died in 2002 at the age of ninety-six. Although she wrote 135 books, most for young readers, Wirt is best known for creating Nancy, a trailblazing and independent young woman who inspired and motivated generations of readers, including some who grew up to become first ladies, U.S. Supreme Court justices and entertainers.

Toledo Lucas County Public Library is home to the Jennifer Fisher/ Nancy Drew Collection and celebrated the ninetieth birthday of the iconic

Opposite, top: Author Mildred Wirt Benson stands next to artwork of Nancy Drew during the eighty-fifth anniversary celebration. *Courtesy of Toledo Lucas County Public Library.*

Opposite, bottom: The Jennifer Fisher/Nancy Drew Collection. *Courtesy of Toledo Lucas County Public Library.*

Above: A display case shows the cherished *Nancy Drew* book collection. *Courtesy of Toledo Lucas County Public Library.*

teen sleuth in 2020. Named for a major fan and collector of artifacts related to *Nancy Drew*, Fisher's collection is housed in the second-floor Children's Library. Two small rooms are used for a rotating display of some of the several thousand items in the collection, from first editions of *Nancy Drew* books and original cover art to merchandise and collectibles beautifully displayed behind elegant glass bookcases. As you wander the richly furnished collection space with its paneled walls and fireplace, you may feel you are walking through a scene from a *Nancy Drew* novel.

A United for Libraries literary landmark plaque stands just outside the exhibit area, dedicated in 2015 in recognition of Wirt's accomplishments. Outside the library is another historic marker that recognizes community and library origins.

Toledo's First High School and Lucas County Public Library Historical Marker

(Ohio Literary Trail Map no. 2)

Location: Outside the library, northwest corner of North Michigan Street and
    Madison Avenue

Latitude: 41.6539300, Longitude: -83.5398560

> *MARKER TEXT*
>
> *Toledo High School opened in 1854 on the site of the city's first log schoolhouse. After an 1895 fire, it was rebuilt and named Central High School. The facility closed in 1914 with the opening of Scott and Waite high schools. It reopened as Woodward Technical School and later became Vocational High. The building was razed in 1938 for construction of the Toledo Public Library.*
>
> *Although Toledo had a subscription library as early as 1838, the city's first free public library opened in 1873 at Madison and Summit streets. The library constructed a building at Madison and Ontario streets in 1890. The Public Works Administration helped finance the present building, which was dedicated on September 4, 1940. The county's three library systems merged in 1970. Marker sponsors: Mercy Hospital of Toledo, Toledo Sesquicentennial Commission, and the Ohio Historical Society.*

House of Four Pillars (Theodore Dreiser) Historical Marker

Maumee, Ohio

(Ohio Literary Trail Map no. 5)

Location: 322 East Broadway Street, Maumee, OH 43537

Latitude: 41.5622600, Longitude: -3.6485330

> *MARKER TEXT*
>
> *Theodore Dreiser wrote in 1900 his famous novel,* Sister Carrie, *in this house. It was built in 1835 and altered to Greek Revival Style in 1844. Dreiser acquired it in 1899. The house possesses most of the features typical of the American "classic temple" including four Doric columns rising the full length of the structure. In 1967 the house was owned by the William M. Hankins family. Marker sponsor: The Ohio Historical Society.*

Author Theodore Dreiser wrote his famous novel in the House of Four Pillars. *Courtesy of Columbus Citizen-Journal Photograph Collection at the Ohio History Connection (P 339).*

In the Area

Maumee Bay State Park, Storybook Trail

Oregon, Ohio

Location: Maumee Bay State Park, Park Road 3 (near the ball court area, behind the resort parking lot), Oregon, OH 43616; for updates, visit ohiodnr. gov/wps/portal/gov/odnr/go-and-do/family-friendly/storybook-trails

If you are traveling in Lucas County with children, stop by Maumee Bay State Park to visit the Storybook Trail, which is about a half mile long and features a fun nature story with a free little library. Posted book panels along the trail tell the story and ask questions about the surrounding area, keeping children engaged in exploration.

Chapter 4

SANDUSKY AND ERIE COUNTIES

Clyde Museum and Sherwood Anderson Historical Marker

Sandusky County, Clyde, Ohio
(Ohio Literary Trail Map no. 1)
Location: The Clyde Museum, 124 West Buckeye Street, Clyde, OH 43310;
    check hours and admission at clydemuseum.org
Historical Marker Location: West Clyde Railroad Plaza, Railroad Street, Clyde
Latitude: 41.3060528, Longitude: -82.9751306

Clyde was home to influential author Sherwood Anderson and the subject of his groundbreaking book Winesburg, Ohio, *about small-town America.*

MARKER TEXT
Sherwood Anderson (1876–1941), author of twenty-seven works, gave up a successful business career in Elyria, Ohio, to concentrate on writing. Born in Camden, Anderson spent his formative years from 1884 to 1895 in Clyde, and in 1919, he published his most notable book, Winesburg, Ohio. *Clyde and small-town Ohio inspired many of its tales. Critics also praised his short story collections, including* The Triumph of the Egg *(1921) and* Death in the Woods *(1933). Commercially successful as a writer, Anderson moved to rural Virginia, where in 1927 he purchased and operated two newspapers while continuing his literary career. Through his writings and encouragement, he was a major influence on a younger*

Left: Author Sherwood Anderson is honored on the streets of Clyde. ©*Bianca Garza.*

Below: *Winesburg, Ohio* was published in 1919 by Sherwood Anderson. ©*Bianca Garza.*

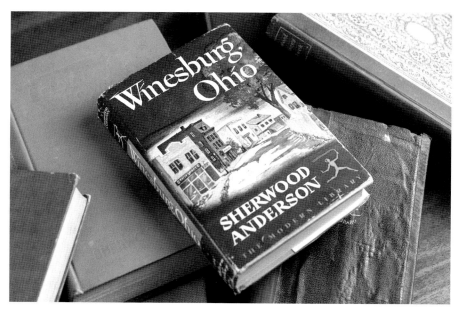

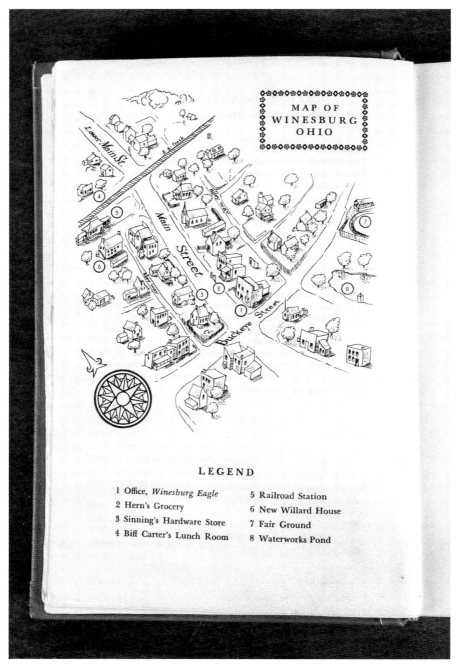

Map of the fictional Winesburg from Sherwood Anderson's *Winesburg, Ohio.* ©*Bianca Garza.*

In 1912, the president of the Public Library Association in Paulding requested funding from philanthropist Andrew Carnegie to build a library in Paulding. At first the Carnegie Corporation of New York refused, stating that it only provided funding to communities with larger populations, but when the Library Association said it would serve the entire county, which had a larger population, the request was granted. As a result, Paulding became the site for the first "county" Carnegie library in the United States, built for a total cost of $40,000. Carnegie provided funding for 2,811 libraries, of which 1,946 were built in the United States. Placed on the National Register of Historic Places in 1984, the Paulding County Carnegie Library continues to service the needs of all citizens of Paulding County. Marker sponsors: Ohio Bicentennial Commission, The Longaberger Company, Paulding County Carnegie Library, and The Ohio Historical Society.

PART III

Northeast Ohio

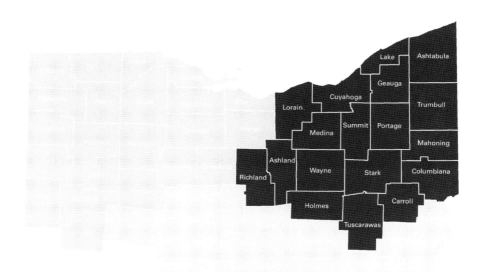

Northeast Ohio region on the Ohio Literary Trail map. *Leslie King design.*

Chapter 6

RICHLAND COUNTY

Louis Bromfield, Malabar Farm and Historical Marker

Richland County, Lucas, Ohio

(Ohio Literary Trail Map no. 10)

Location: Malabar Farm State Park, 4050 Bromfield Road, Lucas, OH 44843; check hours and admission at parks.ohiodnr.gov; the historical marker is located at the south end of visitor parking

Latitude: 40.6515390, Longitude: -82.3987480

Malabar Farm was the home of Pulitzer Prize–winning author and conservationist Louis Bromfield.

MARKER TEXT

Acclaimed author, conservationist and farmer Louis Bromfield was born in Mansfield in 1896. A graduate of the city's schools, he went on to study agriculture at Cornell University in 1914 but left in 1915 to help run his family's farm. In 1916, Bromfield enrolled in Columbia University to study journalism. As America entered World War I, Bromfield enlisted in the U.S. Army Ambulance Service and saw action in seven major European battles. Determined to become a writer, Bromfield finished his education after the war and became a reporter. In 1921, he married Mary Appleton Wood, and they had three daughters. Bromfield's first published novel, The Green Bay Tree *(1924), was a critical and commercial success;*

The Malabar Farm big house hosted the wedding of Humphrey Bogart and Lauren Bacall. *Lindsey Burnett photo.*

his third novel, Early Autumn, *won the Pulitzer Prize in 1927. The Bromfields moved in 1925 to France, where they lived until 1938. In all, he published thirty books and authored numerous stories, articles and screenplays during his writing career.*

The threat of war in Europe and Louis Bromfield's own desire to return to the land of his youth prompted him to purchase three exhausted farms in Pleasant Valley in 1939. He named the estate Malabar Farm after the Malabar Coast of India, the setting of his 1937 book, The Rains Came. *Bromfield then set about to restore the land, putting into practice soil and water conservation techniques that later became widely influential. Devoted to educating farmers and the public about soil and water conservation, Bromfield hosted thousands of visitors at Malabar and expounded his ideas in speeches and columns and over the radio. He also continued to write books, turning to nonfiction to share his experiences. Among these are* Malabar Farm *(1948) and* Out of the Earth *(1950). Bromfield died in 1956, and in the following years, Malabar passed out of family ownership. Malabar Farm became a state park in*

Accolades adorn the entrance to the Toni Morrison Reading Room. *Courtesy of Lorain Public Library System.*

Toni Morrison oversaw the design of the reading room that honors her. *Courtesy of Lorain Public Library System.*

Highlights of the reading room include copies of Morrison's novels *The Bluest Eye* (1970) and *Sula* (1973), personally autographed to the library by Morrison using both her pen name and her real name (Chloe Wofford). Also displayed are correspondence from Morrison, artwork and posters.

Following Morrison's death in New York City in 2019, library administrators oversaw a remodeling of the Toni Morrison Reading Room. It was re-dedicated on February 18, 2020, on what would have been her eighty-ninth birthday.

Visitors may also like these stops related to Toni Morrison: walk through Lakeview Park (Lorain County Metro Parks), which was featured in Morrison's first novel, *The Bluest Eye*; drive by the house where Morrison was born in 1931 (2245 Elyria Avenue), which is a private home; and drive by Washington Irving School, where Morrison attended junior high school (1110 West Fourth Street), which is now a charter school.

Helen Steiner Rice Historical Marker
Lorain County, Lorain, Ohio
(Ohio Literary Trail Map no. 22)
Location: Lakeview Park, West Erie Avenue, Lorain
Latitude: 41.4613830, Longitude: -82.1982500

MARKER TEXT
Helen Steiner Rice was born on May 19, 1900, in Lorain, the daughter of Anna and John Steiner. Demonstrating an early propensity for writing, Helen planned for college, but her father's death during the 1918 Spanish Influenza epidemic kept her working at the Lorain Electric Light and Power Company. In 1929 she married Franklin Rice, a Dayton bank vice president. Following the 1929 stock market crash, she worked for the Gibson Greeting Cards Company in Cincinnati and became editor of verse lines. Known for her words of inspiration, Helen's gift for writing continues to reach millions in her poetry found in modern-day greeting cards and dozens of books. One of America's most prolific poets, she was also an early advocate of women in the workplace. She was elected to the Ohio Women's Hall of Fame in 1992. Helen died April 23, 1981 and was buried next to her parents at the Elmwood Cemetery in Lorain. Marker sponsors: Ohio Bicentennial Commission, The Longaberger Company, Friends of Helen Steiner Rice and Dutch Ink, and The Ohio Historical Society.

Helen Steiner Rice gazebo and historical marker. *Courtesy of Ohio History Connection/remarkableohio.org.*

Ohio Center for the Book/Cleveland Public Library

Cuyahoga County, Cleveland, Ohio

(Ohio Literary Trail Map no. 12)

Location: Cleveland Public Library, 325 Superior Avenue NE, Cleveland, OH
   44114; check hours at cpl.org and programs at ohiocenterforthebook.org

Cleveland Public Library is the home of the Ohio Center for the Book, the designated Ohio Affiliate of the Center for the Book at the Library of Congress and part of a network of Centers for the Book across the country. The center features a growing collection of works by Ohio authors, artists and illustrators that the public can check out.

   In addition to the center's collection, you can browse the vast Cleveland Public Library and discover the Special Collections Room, decorated as it was in the 1920s, which has many fascinating displays. The Main Library lobby architecture and ceiling murals are worth noting, as is the second-floor Superman exhibit, which includes a larger-than-life statue of the Man of Steel himself, in tribute to the character's Cleveland origins.

David L. Deming's Superman guards the second-floor lobby of Cleveland Public Library's Main Library, home to the Ohio Center for the Book and the Literature Department. *Photo by Don Boozer/Cleveland Public Library.*

Additionally, the library is conveniently located near shopping and entertainment including the Rock 'n' Roll Hall of Fame, Great Lakes Science Center and Tower City Center.

Harvey Pekar Literary Landmark Exhibit at Heights Library

Cuyahoga County, Cleveland Heights, Ohio
(Ohio Literary Trail Map no. 16)
Location: Heights Library, Lee Road Branch, 2345 Lee Road, Cleveland
   Heights; check hours at heightslibrary.org

Best known for his *American Splendor* series, Harvey Pekar (1939–2010) spent countless days at Heights Libraries Lee Road branch, researching and writing stories that celebrated his hometown and the common man. Pekar's efforts raised the comic book to a recognized genre.

Harvey Pekar's unique sculpture is an exhibit at the Heights Library. *Courtesy of Heights Libraries.*

The Harvey Pekar statue was donated to Heights Libraries by his widow, Joyce Brabner. She and local artist Justin Coulter designed a warm interactive sculpture. The base of the piece is a real wooden desk with room for people to sit and draw. On top of the desk is a larger-than-life bronze comic book panel, with Pekar stepping out of the bottom of the panel onto the desk. The statue was unveiled at the library as a tribute to the late graphic novelist in 2012. The Cleveland Heights–University Heights Public Library was also dedicated a Literary Landmark in honor of Pekar through United for Libraries.

The lower drawer contains Harvey Pekar memorabilia such as his ID card from the Veterans Administration Center in Cleveland where he worked as a file clerk. The statue is located on the second floor in the adult section between the graphic novel and 'zine collections and the Harvey and Friends Bookshop, a used bookstore run by the Friends of the Heights Libraries. The wall opposite the exhibit has several drawings of Pekar done by friends and admirers.

Home of Superman Historical Marker

Cleveland, Ohio
(Ohio Literary Trail Map no. 24)
Location: Northeast corner St. Clair and East 105th, Cleveland
Latitude: 41.5390750, Longitude: -81.6153530

Marker Text

Jerry Siegel and Joe Shuster, two Glenville High School students imbued with imagination, talent, and passion for science fiction and comics, had their dream become reality in 1932. They created Superman, the first of the superheroes ever to see print. The 1932 prototype was of a villainous superhero. Superman then became the hero who has been called the Action Ace, the Man of Steel, and the Man of Tomorrow.

Although the success of Superman spawned an entire industry, publishers and newspaper syndicates did not originally accept the creation. Superman did not appear until 1938 when he became a lead feature on the cover of Action Comics *No. 1. As co-creators of the most famous of mythical beings, Siegel and Shuster infused popular American culture with one of the most enduring icons of the twentieth century. Superman has appeared in animated series, live-action series, major motion pictures, advertisements, and comic books, where his popularity grows with each generation of readers. Marker sponsors: Ohio Bicentennial Commission, and The Ohio Historical Society.*

James Mercer Langston Hughes Historical Marker

Cuyahoga County, Cleveland, Ohio
(Ohio Literary Trail Map no. 19)
Location: Langston Hughes Branch Library, 10200 Superior Avenue, SE corner
   of Superior Avenue and East Boulevard, Cleveland
Latitude: 41.5213683, Longitude: -81.6175918

Marker Text

One of the most recognized figures of the Harlem Renaissance, Langston Hughes was born in Joplin, Missouri, on February 1, 1902 and moved to Cleveland by the time he was in high school. An avid traveler, he credited his years at Central High School for the inspiration to write and dream. The consummate Renaissance man, Hughes incorporated his love of theater, music, poetry, and literature in his writings. As an activist, he wrote about the racial politics and culture of his day. He was awarded the Spingarn Medal by the NAACP. He published over forty books for both children and adults. Known as the "Poet Laureate of the Negro People," Hughes' most famous poem is "The Negro Speaks of Rivers." Langston died on May 22, 1967, and his remains were interred beneath the commemoratively designed "I've Known Rivers" tile floor in the Schomburg Center for Research in Black Culture in Harlem. Marker sponsors: Ohio Bicentennial Commission, The Greater Cincinnati Foundation, and The Ohio Historical Society.

The Oxcart Library Historical Marker

Cuyahoga County, North Olmsted, Ohio
(Ohio Literary Trail Map no. 20)
Location: At the Butternut Ridge Road entrance to the North Olmsted Public
   Library, 27403 Lorain Road, North Olmsted, OH 44070
Latitude: 41.4122410, Longitude: -81.9257600

MARKER TEXT
In 1829 the citizens of Lenox voted to change the township name to Olmsted as their part of a bargain to acquire 500 books owned by the heirs of Aaron Olmsted. Believed to be the first public library in the Western Reserve, the books were brought from Hartford, Connecticut, by oxcart and were stored in settlers' cabins. The remaining 125 volumes are now housed in the North Olmsted Public Library. Marker sponsors: North Olmsted Landmarks Commission and The Ohio Historical Society.

Books from the original Oxcart Library are on display inside the library. *Courtesy of Ohio History Connection/ remarkableohio.org*

East Cleveland Public Library Historical Marker

Cuyahoga County, East Cleveland, Ohio
(Ohio Literary Trail Map no. 18)
Location: 14101 Euclid Avenue, East Cleveland, OH 44112
Latitude: 41.5283614, Longitude: -81.5844131

MARKER TEXT

On November 12, 1913, the Board of the East Cleveland Public Library met in the office of the East Cleveland Board of Education and plans for a new library were underway. The Carnegie Corporation of New York contributed $35,000 toward the cost of a new building. John D. Rockefeller contributed $3,600 to buy land for future expansion of the library. National Electric Lamp Association, now GE Lighting, donated 129 light bulbs for fixtures in the building. The East Cleveland Public Library stands as an original Carnegie Library dedicated in 1916. The Library officially opened on May 29, 1916. Marker sponsors: Friends of the East Cleveland Public Library, Paul and Karen Dolan, GE Lighting, Mort and Iris November, and The Ohio Historical Society.

Chapter 8

PORTAGE AND STARK COUNTIES

Reinberger Children's Library Center

Portage County, Kent, Ohio

(Ohio Literary Trail Map no. 13)

Location: Kent State University, Third floor of the main University Library, 1125
Risman Drive, Kent, OH 44243; check hours and exhibits at kent.edu/
iSchool/reinberger-childrens-library-center

*Features a collection of more than forty thousand children's books, original
picture book art, posters, movable and historical children's books and more.*

The Center opened in 2003 and has been used as a "demonstration"
children's public and school library center. It is a treasure of the history of
children's publishing and includes historical books in its collection. In 2008,
it expanded due to a donation of more than twenty-two thousand picture
books from the Marantz Picturebook Collection for the Study of Picturebook
Art along with posters, original artwork, ephemera and character toys. Take
time to peruse the collections, including the original picture book art and the
pop-up collection.

While you are at Kent State, stop by the Babar Collection at KSU Library
in the Special Collections department; the May 4 Visitor Center memorial/
museum; Kent State University Museum; and the Design Innovation Hub,
an open-access maker space that takes a cross-disciplinary approach to
making tools, equipment, facilities and idea-sharing available in a one-stop
shop sort of model.

Superman display, Reinberger Children's Library Center. *Courtesy of Reinberger Children's Library Center.*

Reinberger Children's Library Center offers a schedule of author events. *Courtesy of Reinberger Children's Library Center.*

Wick Poetry Center and Poetry Park

Portage County, Kent, Ohio
(Ohio Literary Trail Map no. 13)
Location: Kent State University, 126 South Lincoln Street, Kent, OH 44242;
   check hours and exhibits at kent.edu/wick

One of the premier university poetry centers in the country.

For more than thirty-five years, the Wick Poetry Center has been engaging emerging and established poets and poetry audiences through innovative digital tools, readings, publications, workshops and more. The landscaped Poetry Park (in the heart of the Lefton Esplanade greenway) offers the Joan and Ron Burbick Outdoor Gallery of Traveling Stanzas poetry kiosks. This rotating display of poetry posters adds a lively and interactive component to the park, which includes the Edwin S. Gould Amphitheater, a fifty-seat performance amphitheater, and a twelve-foot bronze sculpture titled *Seated Earth* by artist and Wick Poetry Center cofounder Robert Wick.

Known nationally for its innovative community outreach, the award-winning Traveling Stanzas designs on utility boxes and kiosk displays (seen in the park and community as well as around the world) allow people to see

The landscaped Poetry Park on Lefton Esplanade at Kent State University. *Courtesy of Wick Poetry Center.*

67

A twelve-foot bronze sculpture by Robert Wick is the focal point of the Poetry Park. *Courtesy of Wick Poetry Center.*

Traveling Stanzas appear throughout the Kent community, even on a utility box. *Courtesy of Wick Poetry Center.*

poetry illustrations created by Kent State Visual Communications Design students and hear the poems read by poets in the community. Visitors can follow an online map with audio and GPS directions to all the Traveling Stanzas installations on campus and throughout the Kent downtown area at map.travelingstanzas.com.

Hart Crane Historical Marker

Portage County, Garrettsville, Ohio

(Ohio Literary Trail Map no. 17)

Location: 10688 Freedom Street (southeast corner of Freedom Street and
  Highland Avenue), Garrettsville, OH 44231

Latitude: 41.2829194, Longitude: -81.0978734

> MARKER TEXT
>
> *Harold Hart Crane was born at this site on July 21, 1899, to Grace Hart Crane and Clarence A. Crane, the inventor of Lifesaver Candies, and he lived here until the age of three. "A born poet," according to e.e. cummings,*

Poet Hart Crane's historical marker. *Courtesy of Ohio History Connection/remarkableohio.org.*

Crane dropped out of high school in 1916 and moved from Cleveland to New York City to focus on a literary career. Mainly self-educated, Crane drew his influence from the writings of Walt Whitman and Emily Dickinson. His major work, "The Bridge" (1930), uses the Brooklyn Bridge as a metaphor to celebrate contemporary urban life. Uniquely lyrical in structure and full of imagery, it is considered one of the three major poetic sequences of the first half of the twentieth century, along with T.S. Eliot's "The Waste Land" and William Carlos Williams' "Paterson." Crane died on April 26, 1932. Marker sponsors: Ohio Bicentennial Commission, Greater Cincinnati Foundation, and The Ohio Historical Society.

In the Area

Wingfoot Lake State Park, Storybook Trail

Portage County, Mogadore, Ohio

Location: Goodyear Park Boulevard (just beyond the playground, across from the park office), Mogadore, OH 44260; for details, visit ohiodnr.gov/wps/portal/gov/odnr/go-and-do/family-friendly/storybook-trails

If you are traveling in Portage County with children, stop by Wingfoot Lake State Park to visit the Storybook Trail, which is about a half mile long and features a fun nature story with a free little library. Posted book panels along the trail tell the story and ask questions about the surrounding area, keeping children engaged in exploration.

Haines House Underground Railroad Museum

Stark County, Alliance, Ohio

(Ohio Literary Trail Map no. 9)

Location: 186 West Market Street, Alliance; check hours and admission at haineshouse.org

Setting for nonfiction and historical fiction works on early Underground Railroad history.

Built in stages from 1828 to 1842 by one of the first families to settle in the area, Haines House operated as a station on the Underground Railroad in the years before and during the Civil War. Visitors can view restored

Haines House was built in stages from 1828 to 1842 and operated as a station on the Underground Railroad. *Courtesy of Alliance Area Preservation Society.*

rooms, including a Victorian parlor, an early nineteenth-century kitchen, bedrooms and the attic, where fugitive slaves were hidden. Changing historical displays highlight local preservation, the history of slavery in America and abolitionism.

Jonathan Ridgeway Haines, Sarah Grant Haines and her father, John Grant, builder and original owner of the home, were all members of the Western Anti-Slavery Society, the largest abolitionist organization west of the Alleghenies. Ridgeway served as a vice-president of the organization, and several society meetings were held on the Haines property.

The Haines House has served as a location for both nonfiction and historical fiction works. It is one of numerous locations noted in Ohio's definitive early Underground Railroad history, *The Mysteries of Ohio's Underground Railroads*, by Ohio State University historian Wilbur Siebert. Siebert noted that Alliance was "a hotbed of Abolition."

Ridgeway Haines also figures in some accounts of what is recognized as the story of the last fugitive slave, Sara Lucy Bagby Johnson, who was captured and returned into slavery in Wheeling, Virginia (now West Virginia), just

Visitors to Haines House can see the attic where fugitives stayed. *Courtesy of Alliance Area Preservation Society.*

before the start of the Civil War. Ridgeway has been noted as the leader of a group of abolitionists that unsuccessfully tried to free Lucy by stopping the train returning her to Wheeling at nearby Limaville. It has been recounted in numerous articles and in the play *Lucy Bagby and the Fugitive Slave Law*, by Cleveland's Robin Pease, performed in Ohio and around the country since 2005. More recently, the Haines House served as a location in author Jeffrey Copeland's *Ain't No Harm to Kill the Devil: The Life and Legend of John Fairfield, Abolitionist for Hire* (2015).

PART IV

Central Ohio

Central Ohio region on the Ohio Literary Trail map. *Leslie King design.*

Chapter 10

FRANKLIN COUNTY

Thurber House Museum and Literary Arts Center and Historical Marker

Franklin County, Columbus, Ohio
(Ohio Literary Trail Map no. 25)
Location: 77 Jefferson Avenue, Columbus, OH 43215; for hours, events and
　admission, visit thurberhouse.org
Latitude: 39.9659857, Longitude: -82.9850924

Home of James Thurber, one of the foremost American humorists of the twentieth century.

MARKER TEXT
One of the outstanding American humorists of the twentieth century, James Thurber was born and educated in Columbus. He launched his writing career as a reporter for the Columbus Dispatch *in 1920. In 1927, he began writing for* The New Yorker, *where the first of his distinctively spare cartoons appeared in 1930. Thurber's concise, witty prose spanned a remarkable breadth of genres, including autobiography, fiction, children's fantasy, and modern commentary. Two of his short stories, "The Catbird Seat" and "The Secret Life of Walter Mitty," are among the best-known classics of American literature. Though hampered by failing eyesight, Thurber published almost thirty books in his lifetime. He and his family lived at 77 Jefferson Avenue from 1913 to 1917; the house, listed as*

Above: James Thurber's desk and typewriter. *Courtesy of Thurber House.*

Opposite: The Thurber Dog Garden is located between Thurber House Museum and Literary Arts Center. *Courtesy of Thurber House.*

part of the Jefferson Avenue Historic District on the National Register of Historic Places, became a literary center and museum in 1984. Thurber is buried in Green Lawn Cemetery in Columbus. Marker sponsors: Ohio Bicentennial Commission, The Greater Cincinnati Foundation, and The Ohio Historical Society.

Founded in 1984, Thurber House is a nonprofit literary arts center, James Thurber museum, historic landmark and gathering place for readers, writers and artists of all ages. Visitors can explore the first and second floors of the living museum, play the one-hundred-year-old piano and sit on the furniture. The home is filled with Thurber memorabilia, antique furnishings and informational panels and photographs about the family and Thurber's life. His bedroom contains his original Underwood typewriter, and the bedroom closet is now a repository of signatures from authors who have been hosted by Thurber House. It is appropriate for all ages, and the guided tours are especially suitable for children, as docents can tailor the tour for young age and interests.

Several stories in Thurber's book *My Life and Hard Times* took place in the house, including "The Night the Ghost Got In" and "The Night the

The unicorn sculpture modeled after the creature in Thurber's story "The Unicorn in the Garden" is in the foreground of Thurber House. *Courtesy of Thurber House.*

Bed Fell." Don't miss the dining room and back staircase, where Thurber famously heard ghostly footsteps in 1915. Visitors can walk up the stairs and stand in the very spot where Thurber stood on "The Night the Ghost Got In" (optional: hiding in the same bathroom where Thurber hid from the ghost!). The dining room has been transformed into a museum shop containing one-of-a-kind Thurber-themed items and books.

Finally, the Thurber Dog Garden, located between Thurber House and Literary Arts Center (the multipurpose space), is filled with five larger-than-life Thurber dog statues that provide a unique photo opportunity. Directly across the street, in the elliptical Thurber Park, is a unicorn statue modeled after the creature in Thurber's story "The Unicorn in the Garden" (the full text of which is engraved near the statue).

The Literary Arts Center's events and programs are an important part of the mission of continuing Thurber's legacy. Activities include author events with nationally known and local authors; writing workshops for children and adults; writer residencies; and the presentation of the annual Thurber Prize for American Humor, one of the highest recognitions of humor writing in the United States.

While in the area, you are within walking distance of the Columbus Museum of Art, the giant red "A" at the Columbus College of Art and Design, the Columbus Metropolitan Main Library and Topiary Park, which contains shrubbery depicting the scene from Georges Seurat's famous painting *A Sunday Afternoon on the Island of La Grande Jatte*.

Ohioana Library Association

Franklin County, Columbus, Ohio
(Ohio Literary Trail Map no. 27)
Location: 274 East First Avenue, Suite 300, Columbus, OH 43201; for hours, exhibits and events, visit ohioana.org

Organization dedicated to connecting readers and Ohio writers.

The Ohioana Library collects, preserves and promotes Ohio authors and books related to Ohio topics. The library's holdings include more than fifty thousand books by or about Ohioans, as well as sheet music, biographical files on notable Ohioans, personal papers on Ohio authors and artists, correspondence from Ohio presidents and governors and numerous scrapbooks created by civic and cultural organizations. The room-length shelves are filled with Ohio literature, and highlights include early editions of Harriet Beecher Stowe's *Uncle Tom's Cabin* and Paul Laurence Dunbar's *Oak and Ivy*.

Visitors will see rotating exhibits on display and can peruse materials from the carefully preserved collection in the Martha Kinney Cooper Reading Room. Dedicated in 2001 by Ohio's First Lady Hope Taft, the reading room is decorated with artifacts and keepsakes that illustrate Ohioana's history. Artwork from Ohio artists such as Billy Ireland and Bryan Collier is displayed on the walls.

Ohioana was founded in 1929 by Ohio's First Lady Martha Kinney Cooper, who personally reached out to authors to build the collection. Originally, Ohioana was entirely housed within the Governor's Mansion, the official residence of the Ohio governor. As the collection expanded and required more space, it was rehoused. Today, Ohioana Library is located near downtown Columbus in the renovated Jeffrey Mining Corporate Center, a space it shares with the State Library of Ohio.

In addition to its impressive collection, Ohioana organizes the prestigious Ohioana Awards, which recognize excellence from Ohio authors and

The Ohioana Library Association Martha Kinney Cooper Reading Room welcomes visitors. *Marsha McDevitt-Stredney photo.*

authors of books about Ohio or Ohioans. Presented since 1942, these are the second-oldest literary prizes in the nation. The organization also hosts and maintains the Ohio Literary Trail at ohioana.org.

Columbus Metropolitan Main Library Historical Marker

Franklin County, Columbus, Ohio
(Ohio Literary Trail Map no. 29)
Location: Outside the Library, 96 South Grant Avenue, Columbus, OH 43215
Latitude: 39.9615134, Longitude: -82.9900841

MARKER TEXT
The first tax-supported free public library in Columbus was formed in 1873 and housed in City Hall. In 1901, City Librarian John Pugh petitioned Andrew Carnegie for funding and was granted $200,000. In

*1903, the Swayne home was razed and construction began. The library opened to the public on April 4, 1907. The library's purpose is inscribed on the front of the building—*Bibliotheca Fons Eruditionis: *The library is a fountain of learning; Our Treasures Are Within; and Open to All.*

The home of Judge Noah Swayne was located on this site from 1848 to 1903. Between the 1860s and 1880s, the home served as the Governor's Mansion. Noah Swayne served as a State Representative in 1829 and 1836, U.S. Attorney General for the Ohio district beginning in 1830, and on the first Columbus City Council in 1834. President Abraham Lincoln appointed him as Supreme Court Justice in 1862. In 1902 the house was sold to the City of Columbus for the new library. Marker sponsors: Friends of the Library, Columbus Metropolitan Library, and The Ohio Historical Society.

The Billy Ireland Cartoon Library & Museum

Franklin County, Columbus, Ohio
(Ohio Literary Map no. 26)
Location: The Ohio State University, Sullivant Hall, 1813 North High Street, Columbus, OH 43210; for hours and exhibits, visit cartoons.osu.edu.

Houses the world's largest collection of materials related to cartoons and comics.

The Billy Ireland Cartoon Library & Museum is a unique blend of art, archives and published materials related to cartoons and comic art. Visitors will see how comics reflect our culture and society. The world's largest collection includes 2.5 million newspaper comic strip clippings, more than 30,000 pieces of original art, 67,000 serials and comic books, more than 45,000 graphic novels and books, more than 6,000 boxes of archival material and an extensive collection of manga (Japanese comics).

Visitors can browse rotating exhibits in museum galleries, as well as the "Treasures from the Collection" exhibit that provides an overview of the history of comics. A private donation supported the commission of the two beautiful art glass windows in Sullivant Hall showcasing Ireland's cartoons from the *Columbus Dispatch*.

Established in 1977 in two converted classrooms with a founding gift of artwork and papers from cartoonist and Ohio State alumnus Milton Caniff, the museum has grown through acquisitions and donations to become the largest and most comprehensive academic research facility documenting

Visitors enjoy exhibits at the Billie Ireland Cartoon Library & Museum. *Jodi Miller Photography.*

Displays provide an overview of the history of comics. *Jodi Miller Photography.*

Top: The Wagnalls Memorial Library room. *Courtesy of Wagnalls Memorial Library.*

Bottom: Exterior of Wagnalls Memorial Library. *Courtesy of Wagnalls Memorial Library.*

her daughter and helped her husband in all of his endeavors. Mabel, an author and concert pianist, knew it had always been Anna's dream to do something for her home village and to provide opportunities not available to her as a child. By giving Lithopolis a library, theater and event center, Mabel fulfilled her mother's dream.

The children's room at the Wagnalls Memorial Library. *Courtesy of Wagnalls Memorial Library.*

In addition to traditional library services, the Wagnalls hosts family-friendly events such as an arts and entertainment festival, a magical-themed Yule Ball and the adult Roaring Twenties Great Gatsby Party.

The children's library fills an entire level of the building with a fun, colorful, inviting space for children and their caretakers and features a creative play space suitable for ages between two and twelve. The train station and corral were built by a local craftsman whose children enjoyed story time here.

For garden aficionados, it is best to come in the warmer months, when the Walker-Hecox-Hickle gardens (maintained by the Fairfield County Master Gardeners) are in bloom. Visitors can stroll the pathways and see rock sculptures, including stone birdhouses, built by a local doctor.

Nearby, the village of Lithopolis and the surrounding countryside feature quaint shops and eateries, parks and the historic Rock Mill. Annual village events include the Memorial Day Fish Fry and Car Show and the Honeyfest in September.

Chapter 12

MORROW, KNOX AND DELAWARE COUNTIES

Dawn Powell Historical Marker
Morrow County, Mount Gilead, Ohio
(Ohio Literary Trail Map no. 30)
Location: Mount Gilead Public Library on Walnut Street side, 41 East High
   Street, Mount Gilead, OH 43338
Latitude: 40.5488660, Longitude: -82.8272220

MARKER TEXT
The author of fifteen novels, ten plays, and more than 100 stories, Dawn Powell was born in 1896 in Mount Gilead at 53 West North Street and grew up in Shelby. She graduated from Lake Erie College in Painesville and moved to New York in 1918. Although some of her early works, such as She Walks in Beauty *(1928) and* The Bride's House *(1929), draw from her life in small-town Ohio, she is best known for her satiric portrayals of life in New York, including* A Time to Be Born *(1942) and* The Wicked Pavilion *(1954). Often compared to Dorothy Parker and associated with contemporaries John Dos Passos, Edmund Wilson, Ernest Hemingway, and Gore Vidal, Powell received the Marjorie Peabody Waite Award for lifelong achievement in literature in 1964. She died in New York in 1965. Marker sponsors: Ohio Bicentennial Commission, The Longaberger Company, Mount Gilead Public Library Association, and The Ohio Historical Society.*

John Crowe Ransom and the *Kenyon Review* Historical Marker

Knox County, Gambier, Ohio
(Ohio Literary Trail Map no. 31)
Location: Kenyon College, Finn House, 102 West Wiggin Street, Gambier, OH
  43022
Latitude: 40.3760860, Longitude: -82.3983250

Marker Text

In 1938 the president of Kenyon College, Gordon Keith Chalmers, brought one of the nation's most distinguished poets and critics, John Crowe Ransom, to the Gambier Hill. Chalmers brought Ransom to Kenyon College to create a distinguished literary review. With its first appearance late in 1938, The Kenyon Review *would become one of the most influential and honored literary magazines in America. Among the authors Ransom published during his two decades as editor were Robert Penn Warren, William Empson, Flannery O'Connor, Doris Lessing, Robert Lowell, and Randall Jarrell.* The Kenyon Review *also became closely identified with the "New Criticism," a method of interpreting literature that influenced succeeding generations of readers and teachers around the world.*

Aspiring writers made pilgrimages to Gambier to work with John Crowe Ransom. Poet Robert Lowell transferred from Harvard to Kenyon College to study with Ransom in 1938. Peter Taylor, one of America's greatest short story writers, soon appeared as well and became Lowell's roommate in Douglass House. Others there included Randall Jarrell and Robie Macauley. Along with F.O. Matthiessen and Lionel Trilling, Ransom founded the Kenyon School of English in 1948. The school operated for several summers and brought together students for the study of literature at the graduate level. In the 1940s and '50s, talented younger writers continued to arrive, including E.L. Doctorow and James Wright. Marker sponsors: Ohio Bicentennial Commission, and The Ohio Historical Society.

In the Area

Alum Creek State Park, Storybook Trail

Delaware County, Lewis Center, Ohio

Location: Alum Creek State Park Beach (north side), 3400 Lewis Center Road, Lewis Center, OH 43035; for details, visit ohiodnr.gov/wps/portal/gov/odnr/go-and-do/family-friendly/storybook-trails

If you are traveling in Delaware County with children, stop by Alum Creek State Park to visit the Storybook Trail, which is about a half mile long and features a fun nature story with a free little library. Posted book panels along the trail tell the story and ask questions about the surrounding area, keeping children engaged in exploration.

PART V

Southwest Ohio

Southwest Ohio region on the Ohio Literary Trail map. *Leslie King design.*

Chapter 13

HAMILTON AND BUTLER COUNTIES

Harriet Beecher Stowe House and Historical Marker
Hamilton County, Cincinnati, Ohio
(Ohio Literary Trail Map no. 33)
Location: 2950 Gilbert Avenue, Cincinnati, OH 45206; for hours, tours and
    fees, visit stowehousecincy.org
Latitude: 39.1330910, Longitude: -84.4876740

Historic home of the author of Uncle Tom's Cabin.

The Harriet Beecher Stowe House is a historical and cultural site focusing on the author and her legacy of humanity and social justice. Tours of the house focus on her life, family and experiences while living in Cincinnati, which influenced her writing *Uncle Tom's Cabin*, as well as the role of the house in later years. The Educational Center has activities for children visiting the house, including writing with a simulated quill and ink, practicing on a slate with chalk and perusing nineteenth-century books.

> MARKER TEXT
> *Harriet Beecher Stowe was born in Litchfield, Connecticut, in 1811 and moved to Cincinnati in 1832 when her father, prominent Congregational minister Lyman Beecher, became the pastor of the city's Second Presbyterian Church and president of Lane Theological Seminary. Married to Calvin*

Above: Harriet Beecher Stowe House. *Courtesy of Ohio History Connection.*

Right: Harriet Beecher Stowe portrait. *Courtesy of Ohio History Connection (AL00530).*

Opposite, top: Inside Stowe House. *Courtesy of Harriet Beecher Stowe House.*

Opposite, bottom: Children enjoy displays designed for young visitors. *Courtesy of Harriet Beecher Stowe House.*

E. Stowe in 1836, she bore six of the couple's seven children while living here. Life in the city provided Stowe with the firsthand accounts about the evils of slavery. Already a published writer, she drew on these experiences and the death of her infant son Charley in 1849 to write Uncle Tom's Cabin. *Published in book form in 1852,* Uncle Tom's Cabin *almost single-handedly popularized the cause of antislavery, made Stowe famous and remains an icon of the American antislavery movement. A prolific*

writer, Stowe wrote one book per year for nearly thirty years of her life. After moving from Cincinnati in 1850, the Stowes lived in Brunswick, Maine; Andover, Massachusetts; and Hartford, Connecticut, where she died in 1896. Marker sponsors: Ohio Bicentennial Commission, The Cincinnati Foundation, and The Ohio Historical Society.

Cincinnati played a large part in the abolitionist movement, and a number of key figures lived along Gilbert Avenue at various times, including the country's first female physician, Elizabeth Blackwell. Visitors can take a walking tour of Gilbert Avenue and learn more about the history and impact on the antislavery movement.

The Mercantile Library

Hamilton County, Cincinnati, Ohio
(Ohio Literary Trail Map no. 36)
Location: 414 Walnut Street #1100, Cincinnati, OH 45202; for hours and
   details, visit mercantilelibrary.com

The oldest continuously operating library west of Philadelphia.

Founded in 1835 by a group of young Cincinnati merchants who pooled their resources, books and talents, the Mercantile Library is the oldest membership library west of the Alleghenies. While the address has been the same since 1940, it has occupied four different buildings due to fire and other circumstances. The two-story stacks with glass floors are original to 1904, when the current space was built. Over the years, they have collected works of art and hosted noted speakers and authors, including Herman Melville, Ralph Waldo Emerson, Harriet Beecher Stowe, Toni Morrison, Margaret Atwood and more. Today, it is one of nearly two dozen surviving membership libraries in the United States, and it continues to connect people with authors, speakers and discussion groups.

The collection contains more than eighty thousand volumes and covers a broad range of subjects. Among its most notable literary works are first editions of Charles Dickens's *Our Mutual Friend* and *Dombey and Son*, as well as a 1479 folio-sized Bible written in Latin and published in Nuremburg, Germany.

Because the library predated public art institutions, it collected art and rare cultural works. Holdings include an original marble bust of President

Mercantile Library reading room. *Bryan Loar photo*.

The sculpture *Silence* greets visitors to the Mercantile Library. *Phil Armstrong/Mercantile Library*.

William H. Harrison, a bust of Abraham Lincoln and a marble replica of Joseph Mozier's *Silence* that stands at the entrance, as well as presidential letters from George Washington and John Adams and much more.

VISITORS TO FOUNTAIN SQUARE will additionally see the Tyler Davidson Fountain and, east of that, the Water Wall, engraved with the last stanza of Henry Wadsworth Longfellow's *Catawba Wine*, which memorialized Cincinnati as the Queen City. Also nearby are the Taft Art Museum, Cincinnati Museum Center and the Contemporary Arts Center.

The Jacob Rader Marcus Center of the American Jewish Archives Historical Marker

Hamilton County, Cincinnati, Ohio
(Ohio Literary Trail Map no. 46)
Location: Outside the Center at 3101 Clifton Avenue, Cincinnati, OH 45220
Latitude: 39.1382350, Longitude: -84.5202780

> MARKER TEXT
> Dr. Jacob Rader Marcus (1896–1995), pioneering historian of the American Jew, founded the American Jewish Archives (AJA) in Cincinnati in 1947. In the aftermath of World War II and the brutal destruction of European Jewry, Marcus anticipated the need to establish a central repository dedicated to preserving the history of North American Jewry. The AJA, which began with a few boxes of documents, has become one of the world's largest catalogued collections of primary source material on the history of American Jewry. An international community of scholars, researchers, and students utilizes the AJA's vast archival holdings. Marker sponsors: Ohio Bicentennial Commission, The International Paper Company Foundation, and The Ohio Historical Society.

Public Library of Cincinnati and Hamilton County Historical Marker

Hamilton County, Cincinnati, Ohio
(Ohio Literary Trail Map no. 48)
Location: 800 Vine Street, on the east side of Vine Street between Eighth Street and Ninth Street, Cincinnati
Latitude: 39.1049750, Longitude: -84.5137540

MARKER TEXT

Among the first in America, Cincinnati's public library dates from March 14, 1853. A public reading room opened in 1856, but funding remained a problem until 1867, when local school board president Rufus King II secured legislation for a renamed Cincinnati Public Library. In 1869, King lured leading librarian William Frederick Poole to organize Cincinnati as a national model for the growing public library movement. Poole designed nineteenth-century America's most advanced library at 629 Vine Street, which fully opened in 1874. Becoming a countywide system in 1898, the Public Library of Cincinnati and Hamilton County was a pioneer in the twentieth century with special services for the blind and for children, bookmobile services, and circulation of audiovisual materials.

The Public Library of Cincinnati and Hamilton County's new Main Library that opened in 1955 at the corner of Eighth and Vine was post-war America's first major central public library. It was dedicated as a memorial to the servicemen and women from Hamilton County killed while in the Armed Forces. Its boldly modern "International Style" exterior was the work of local architect Woodie Garber, and its consumer-oriented "department store of knowledge" layout was the creation of Librarian

The Amelia Valerio Weinberg Memorial Fountain is known as the "Books Fountain."
Courtesy of Cincinnati & Hamilton County Public Library.

Carl Vitz. The 1955 "New Main" garnered national attention and architectural praise for its sidewalk "store" entrance, generous use of glass, bright colors, rooftop terraces, and serpentine brick garden wall. Additions in 1982 and 1997 quadrupled the size of the Main Library. Marker sponsors: Library Gift Trust Fund and The Ohio Historical Society.

In the Area

Amelia Valerio Weinberg Memorial Fountain at Cincinnati and Hamilton Public Library

Located on the Vine Street plaza in front of the Main Library and affectionately known as the "Books Fountain," this memorial was conceived and executed by former Cincinnati sculptor Michael Frasca and depicts a collection of old bound books with a central waterfall running into a pool. The fountain, dedicated in 1990, was made possible by a bequest to the library for the construction of a fountain when Weinberg died in 1980.

The McCloskey Museum

Butler County, Hamilton, Ohio
(Ohio Literary Trail Map no. 44)
Location: Heritage Hall, 20 High Street, Hamilton; for details, visit
   hamiltonheritagehall.org

Honors national award-winning children's author and illustrator Robert McCloskey.

Two-time Caldecott Award winner Robert McCloskey (1914–2003) was born in Hamilton, and his first book, *Lentil*, featured several Hamilton scenes, including the Hamilton Lane Library, which he visited often as a child. Published by Viking in 1940, it told the story of a boy much like himself, and Hamilton's midwestern influence is evident in his books. His creative expression began in art, drawing, painting and sculpture, including carving a totem pole while he was a YMCA camp counselor.

In the lobby of Heritage Hall, you will see the timeline of McCloskey's life, including the totem pole that McCloskey carved while working as a teenager at Camp Campbell Gard. On the first floor of Heritage Hall, the McCloskey Museum houses a wide collection of original paintings and

Right: William Holmes McGuffey portrait. *Courtesy of Ohio History Connection (AL03317).*

Below: William Holmes McGuffey House. *Courtesy of Ohio History Connection/remarkableohio.org.*

sponsors: Ohio Bicentennial Commission, The Longaberger Company, Miami University, and The Ohio Historical Society.

The museum houses one of the nation's most complete collections of *McGuffey Readers*, as well as other common school texts. A variety of educational artifacts—including McGuffey's personal secretary desk, lectern and Reading Charts published in 1880—is on display in the museum library. Visitors are given guided tours by trained staff, students and docents. There is no admission charge, although donations are welcome.

Percy MacKaye and "The Poet's Shack" Historical Marker
Butler County, Oxford, Ohio
(Ohio Literary Trail Map no. 45)
Location: Northwest section of Bishop Circle (Bishop Woods), Oxford, OH
  45056
Latitude: 39.5090370, Longitude: -84.7326160

MARKER TEXT
"The Poet's Shack" was built as a writing studio for the prolific poet Percy MacKaye, who held the position of writer-in-residence at Miami University from 1920 to 1924. MacKaye requested a writing studio in the woods, a simple shack with a fire where faculty and students could gather to talk with the poet or hear his newest works. MacKaye's studio was built on Miami's lower campus—now known as Bishop Woods after first president Robert Hamilton Bishop—where Upham Hall stands today. Students called the structure "The Poet's Shack."

Percy MacKaye (1875–1956) was a poet and dramatist elected to the National Institute of Arts and Letters in 1914. From 1920 to 1924, MacKaye held the position of writer-in-residence at Miami University, the first position of its kind at any American university. Robert Frost praised MacKaye for advocating "to get his fellow poets all fellowships at the universities." During his time in "The Poet's Shack," MacKaye produced the well-known poems "The Trees of Miami" and "An Ode to the Universities," as well as This Fine Pretty World: A Comedy of the Kentucky Mountains *(1924), a play performed on New York's Broadway throughout the 1920s. Marker sponsors: John W. Altman Charitable Foundation, Miami University, and The Ohio History Connection.*

Chapter 14

MONTGOMERY AND GREENE COUNTIES

Paul Laurence Dunbar House and State Memorial and Historical Marker

Montgomery County, Dayton, Ohio

(Ohio Literary Trail Map no. 34)

Location: 219 North Paul Laurence Dunbar Street, Dayton, OH 45407; for hours, visit nps.gov/daav/planyourvisit/paul-laurence-dunbar-house-historic-site.htm

The first African American artist to achieve prominence as a poet.

MARKER TEXT

The first African American to achieve prominence as a poet, Paul Laurence Dunbar was born and raised in Dayton, the son of former slaves. Working as an elevator operator while he established himself as a writer, Dunbar published his first book of poems, Oak and Ivy, *in 1893. His third collection,* Lyrics of a Lowly Life *(1896), with an introduction by another Ohio-born author, William Dean Howells, gained Dunbar widespread critical acclaim and popular recognition. Widely published in contemporary journals and literary magazines, Dunbar employed both turn-of-the-century African American dialect and standard English verse to give a voice to the themes of everyday discrimination and struggles for racial equality. Tuberculosis cut his life short at age thirty-three. Dunbar's body of*

Paul Laurence Dunbar. *Courtesy of Ohio History Connection (AL03381).*

work includes twelve volumes of poetry, four books of short stories, a play, and five novels. Marker sponsors: Ohio Bicentennial Commission and The Ohio Historical Society.

After attaining fame, Dunbar purchased the house for his mother, Matilda, in 1904, and he lived there and continued to write until his death in 1906. He completed his last works in the house, and Matilda lived there until her death in 1934. The restored Dunbar House appears today much as it did at the time of the poet's death and is a trip back in time due to its preservation. The visitor center entrance is located on Edison Street (just around the corner from the Dunbar house), where you can view a movie and see artifacts and exhibits dedicated to the life of Dunbar before you tour the house.

Virginia Hamilton Historical Marker

Greene County, Yellow Springs, Ohio
(Ohio Literary Trail Map no. 41)
Location: 740 Dayton Street, Yellow Springs, OH 45387
Latitude: 39.8039862, Longitude: -83.8900117

MARKER TEXT

Virginia Hamilton was an author who was born in Yellow Springs in 1934, living and writing there for much of her life. She referred to her works as "Liberation Literature," focusing on the struggles and journeys of African Americans. Hamilton published more than forty books in a variety of genres, including realistic novels, science fiction, picture books, folktales and mysteries. Some of her most beloved titles include The House of Dies Drear, M.C. Higgins the Great, Her Stories, *and* The People Could Fly. *Her books have had a profound influence on the study of race throughout American history, the achievements of African Americans, and the ramifications of racism. Hamilton received numerous awards for her writing before passing-away in 2002. Her work is enshrined at the Library of Congress in Washington, D.C. Marker sponsors: Dayton Regional STEM School, Greene County Public Library, Yellow Springs Community Foundation, and The Ohio History Connection.*

In the Area

John Bryan State Park, Storybook Trail

Greene County, Yellow Springs, Ohio
Location: 3790 Bryan Park Road (behind the playground), Yellow Springs, OH 45387; for details, visit ohiodnr.gov/wps/portal/gov/odnr/go-and-do/family-friendly/storybook-trails

If you are traveling in Greene County with children, stop by John Bryan State Park to visit the Storybook Trail, which is about a half mile long and features a fun nature story with a free little library. Posted book panels along the trail tell the story and ask questions about the surrounding area, keeping children engaged in exploration.

Chapter 15

BROWN, HIGHLAND AND CLINTON COUNTIES

The Rankin House

Brown County, Ripley, Ohio

(Ohio Literary Trail Map no. 37)

Location: 6152 Rankin Road (turn up the hill at 500 North Second Street),
   Ripley, OH 45167; for hours and details, visit ripleyohio.net/htm/rankin.htm

National Historic Landmark home and original stop on Underground Railroad.

Reverend John Rankin was minister of Ripley's Presbyterian Church for forty-four years. In 1825, he built the house on Liberty Hill overlooking the Ohio River. With its proximity to the river and Rankin's opposition to slavery, it was an ideal first stopping point on the Underground Railroad. The Rankin family, which included thirteen children, was proud of never losing a "passenger," and it is thought that most of the two thousand escaped slaves who traveled through Ripley stopped at the house.

Rankin wrote a series of letters to the editor of the local newspaper articulating antislavery views and denouncing slavery. In addition, he wrote *Letters on American Slavery* in 1826, which became standard reading for abolitionists across the county. His preaching and writing inspired others to join the antislavery cause. Harriet Beecher Stowe heard Rankin's account of one slave who carried her child across the icy river and later included it in her book *Uncle Tom's Cabin*.

The parlor at Rankin House. *Courtesy of Ohio History Connection.*

The Rankin House with steps. *Courtesy of Ohio History Connection.*

Rankin House bedroom. *Courtesy of the Ohio History Connection.*

One hundred steps led from Ripley to the house on the hill, and they are still accessible today. The house is a National Historic Landmark, and much of the woodwork and several personal items—including the Rankin family Bible—are on display. Historic Ripley is a picturesque village on the Ohio River Scenic Byway, east of Cincinnati. The area offers many tourist attractions, museums, events, wineries, covered bridges and more.

Albert Nelson Marquis/Who's Who Historical Marker

Brown County, Decatur, Ohio

(Ohio Literary Trail Map no. 47)

Location: Park on Main Street/OH 125 (located on back of Historic Decatur marker), southeast corner of Main Street and Eagle Street/Huff Hill Road, Decatur, OH 45115

Latitude: 38.8152690, Longitude: -83.7039150

MARKER TEXT

Born in Decatur and reared in nearby Hamersville, Albert Nelson Marquis (1855–1943) began his own publishing company in Cincinnati at age twenty-one. In 1884 he moved A.N. Marquis and Co. to Chicago, where he specialized in business directories. Marquis published the first edition of Who's Who in America *in 1899. Immediately successful, the* Big Red Book *listed biographical information about nationally significant individuals and inspired many similar topical references. Marquis was editor-in-chief until 1940.* Who's Who in America *remains a standard reference for information about accomplished living Americans. Marker sponsors: Decatur Bicentennial Committee, Byrd Township Trustees, and The Ohio Historical Society.*

Milton Caniff Historical Marker

Highland County, Hillsboro, Ohio
(Ohio Literary Trail Map no. 40)
Location: Highland County District Library, 10 Willettsville Pike, Hillsboro, OH 45133
Latitude: 39.2036260, Longitude: -83.6210820

MARKER TEXT
Creator of some of America's favorite cartoon characters, Milton Caniff was born in Hillsboro in 1907 and graduated from Ohio State University in 1930. He created his first comic strip in 1932 for the Associated Press

Milton Caniff. *Courtesy of Billy Ireland Cartoon Library & Museum.*

Syndicate, and in 1934 introduced Terry and the Pirates, *an innovative serial adventure featuring believable characters drawn with unprecedented realism. Enormously popular through the World War II years for both* Terry *and the comic strip* Male Call, *which he created for the U.S. military's Camp Newspaper Service, Caniff subsequently introduced* Steve Canyon *in 1947.* Steve Canyon *ran for forty-one years until Caniff's death in 1988. Credited with influencing generations of successful cartoonists, Caniff brought adventure, suspense, and sensuality to what had been largely a medium for humor and melodrama. Marker sponsors: Ohio Bicentennial Commission and The Ohio Historical Society.*

Wilmington Library Historical Marker

Clinton County, Wilmington, Ohio
(Ohio Literary Trail Map no. 50)
Location: Wilmington Public Library of Clinton County, 268 North South Street,
   Wilmington, OH 45177
Latitude: 39.4492613, Longitude: -83.8278751

MARKER TEXT
The Wilmington Public Library of Clinton County, one of 111 Carnegie libraries in Ohio, opened its doors to readers on June 30, 1904. A $12,500 gift from steel magnate and philanthropist Andrew Carnegie financed construction of the original 3,360-square-foot building. The community provided the building site, formerly known as Martin Field, and pledged tax funds for the library's ongoing operation and maintenance. Expansions and modernizations have incorporated the original building and preserved its historic architectural style. "A library outranks any other thing a community can do to benefit its people," Andrew Carnegie. Marker sponsors: Wilmington Public Library of Clinton County and The Ohio History Connection.

PART VI

Southeast Ohio

Southeast Ohio region on the Ohio Literary Trail map. *Leslie King design.*

Chapter 16

MUSKINGUM, MORGAN, ATHENS AND WASHINGTON COUNTIES

Zane Grey and National Road Museum and Historical Marker
Muskingum County, Norwich, Ohio
(Ohio Literary Trail Map no. 52)
Location: 8850 East Pike, Norwich, OH 43701; for hours and admission, visit
 ohiohistory.org

Zane Grey Historical Marker
(Ohio Literary Trail Map no. 52)
Location: 705 Convers Avenue, Zanesville, OH 43701
Latitude: 39.9503760, Longitude: -82.0126040

Zane Grey established the western as an American literary genre and is known as the "Father of the Western Novel."

This facility includes three different museums in one location: one honors Zane Grey, a second shows off the historic National Road and a third is dedicated to local art including pottery, ceramics and tile.

The Zane Grey portion of the museum is dedicated to the writer and adventurer's life, books and movies. Grey's study is re-created in the museum, and the display includes many manuscripts and other personal memorabilia. The National Road, U.S. 40, was known as "the Main Street of America" and America's busiest road connecting the East Coast and the western frontier in the early nineteenth century. This museum section features

National Road and Zane Grey Museum transportation display. *Courtesy of Ohio History Connection.*

Zane Grey Museum exhibit. *Courtesy of Museum Association of East Muskingum.*

Zane Grey correcting a manuscript. *Courtesy of Ohio History Connection (AL04956).*

vintage carriages, automobiles, a Conestoga wagon and a 135-foot diorama showing the progression of the road's development. The smallest section of the museum displays glass and pottery art from an era when Zanesville-area companies were major producers.

> *Marker Text*
> *Born Pearl Zane Gray in 1872 at this site and raised in Zanesville, author Zane Grey established the western novel as a twentieth-century American literary genre.* [During his late teens, he sought to distance himself from a family scandal and changed the spelling of his last name.] *Trained as a dentist and practicing in New York City, Grey began writing full time following his marriage in 1905 to Lina Elise "Dolly" Roth, who served as his editor and agent. Grey's novels featured rich western imagery and highly romanticized plots, often with pointed moral overtones, inspiring scores of imitators. Of his more than sixty books,* Riders of the Purple Sage *(1912) is his best-known work. Many of Grey's novels were made*

into movies in the 1920s and '30s. In addition, Grey was the holder of ten world records for large game fishing, an avocation he pursued when not writing. He died in 1939 at his home in Altadena, California. Marker sponsors: Ohio Bicentennial Commission, The Longaberger Company, The Business Advocate Inc., and The Ohio Historical Society.

Additionally, make a plan to visit the John and Annie Glenn Museum in nearby New Concord, honoring astronaut and senator John Glenn and his wife. Like the Zane Grey Museum, this historical site and museum is a site partner of the Ohio History Connection.

In the Area

Dillon State Park, Storybook Trail

Muskingum County, Zanesville, Ohio

Location: Dillon State Park Beach (Black Locust Loop, behind the ball court area), 5265 Dillon Hills Drive, Zanesville, OH 43830; for details, visit ohiodnr.gov/wps/portal/gov/odnr/go-and-do/family-friendly/ storybook-trails

If you are traveling in Muskingum County with children, stop by Dillon State Park to visit the Storybook Trail, which is about a half mile long and features a fun nature story with a free little library. Posted book panels along the trail tell the story and ask questions about the surrounding area, keeping children engaged in exploration.

Left: Visitors to Dillon State Park's Storybook Trail are greeted with a special entrance. *Courtesy of Stephanie O'Grady.*

Opposite: Child-size story panels along the Dillon Storybook Trail feature pages from *Miss Maple's Seeds* by Eliza Wheeler. *Courtesy of Stephanie O'Grady.*

Ohio Department of Natural Resources (ODNR) opened its first State Park Storybook Trail in October 2019, and four more opened in 2020. In partnership with the Ohio Governor's Imagination Library and Dolly Parton's Imagination Library, ODNR launched the program to promote reading and a love of the outdoors for families and their youngest members.

Each trail features a different story, and families can walk their way through some of Ohio's most picturesque trails while learning about different aspects of nature from the books and authors who were inspired by nature. All five of the trails are included in this book, with one in each of Ohio's regions; new trails will be added in the future.

Frances Dana Gage Historical Marker

Morgan County, McConnelsville, Ohio
(Ohio Literary Trail Map no. 55)
Location: Just north of 210 North Kennebec Avenue (up small walkway north of Church of Gospel Ministry), McConnelsville, OH 43756
Latitude: 39.4425984, Longitude: -81.4587000

MARKER TEXT
One of Ohio's earliest proponents of women's rights, Frances Dana Gage (1808–1884) was born in Marietta and married McConnelsville attorney James L. Gage in 1829. She immersed herself in the major social issues of the day—temperance, abolition, and universal suffrage—while raising eight children. At a women's rights convention in 1850, Gage gained national

Frances Dana Gage portrait. *Courtesy of Ohio History Connection (AL04122).*

attention by proposing that the words "white" and "men" be removed from Ohio's constitution. She later served as the editor of an Ohio agricultural journal, as an educator for newly emancipated African Americans, and wrote children's tales under the pen name "Aunt Fanny." An enormously influential woman, Gage led the way for Ohio's next generation of social activists. Marker sponsors: Ohio Bicentennial Commission, The International Paper Company Foundation, and The Ohio Historical Society.

Western Library Association, 1804—Coonskin Library Historical Marker

Athens County, Amesville, Ohio
(Ohio Literary Trail Map no. 60)
Location: Village Park, 1 State Street/OH 550, Amesville, OH 45711
Latitude: 39.4002330, Longitude: -81.9558860

Marker Text
In the years leading to Ohio's statehood in 1803, Ames Township citizens decided to establish a stock-owned circulating library. Since cash was scarce during Ohio's frontier era, some citizens paid for their $2.50 shares by the

sale of animal pelts, which were taken to Boston for sale in the spring of 1804 by merchant Samuel Brown. There he acquired fifty-one volumes, primarily books on history, religion, travel, and biography, as the first accessions for the Western Library Association. Senator Thomas Ewing later related that he paid his share with ten raccoon skins, thus suggesting the collection's popular name "the Coonskin Library." Judge Ephraim Cutler was the first of many librarians who kept the library until 1861. Marker sponsors: Ohio Bicentennial Commission, The International Paper Company Foundation, and The Ohio Historical Society.

Putnam Family Library/Belpre Farmers' Library Historical Marker

Washington County, Belpre, Ohio
(Ohio Literary Trail Map no. 57)
Location: 2012 Washington Boulevard, Belpre, OH 45714
Latitude: 39.2778140, Longitude: -81.6030760

MARKER TEXT

As a shareholder of the United Library Association in Pomfret, Connecticut, General Israel Putnam amassed a large collection of books, which was called the Putnam Family Library. The collection was divided among his heirs after his death in 1790. His son, Colonel Israel Putnam, brought part of that collection with him to Washington County, Ohio, in 1795. Education was a foremost concern to settlers in the Ohio Country and was reinforced in article three of the Northwest Ordinance of 1787. Accordingly, the Putnam family's collection circulated among neighbors and provided the means of education for the people of Belpre and surrounding communities. By 1796, a group of subscribers, paying ten dollars a share, fully organized a public library. Later known as the Belpre Farmers' Library, it was the first library established in the Northwest Territory. The library operated under the management of the shareholders until 1815. Marker sponsors: Ohio Bicentennial Commission, The Longaberger Company, Belpre Historical Society, Washington County Public Library, and The Ohio Historical Society.

Chapter 17

HOCKING, ROSS
AND MEIGS COUNTIES

Grandma Gatewood Memorial Trail

Hocking County, South Bloomingville, Ohio
(Ohio Literary Trail Map no. 53)
Location: Hocking Hills State Park; this six-mile trail runs through Old Man's
    Cave (19852 State Route 664, Logan), Cedar Falls and the Ash Cave (State
    Route 56, just west of State Route 374, South Bloomingville) ; for park/trail
    conditions, visit parks.ohiodnr.gov/hockinghills

*"Grandma" Emma Gatewood was the first woman to hike the entire
Appalachian Trail solo in 1955.*

Ohioan Emma Gatewood is a legend, inspiring numerous books for children
and adults, as well as outdoor exploration. In 1955, at age sixty-seven, she
became the first woman to hike the entire Appalachian Trail by herself,
covering the 2,050-mile route from Georgia to Maine in one season. The
mother of eleven and grandmother carried only a small sack. It was later
revealed that she was a thirty-year survivor of spousal abuse who enjoyed
hiking as an escape. She became an inspiration to writers, women and
hikers, as well as senior citizens.

The Grandma Gatewood Memorial Trail extends from Old Man's
Cave to Ash Cave, two of Hocking Hills State Park's most famous natural
landmarks. The inspiring view and forestry on the trail provide a true sense

Ash Cave on the Grandma Gatewood Memorial Trail is an inspiring hike, even in the winter. *Courtesy of Ohio Department of Natural Resources (ODNR).*

Old Man's Cave. *Courtesy of Ohio Department of Natural Resources (ODNR).*

Upper Falls on the trail. *Courtesy of Ohio Department of Natural Resources (ODNR).*

of Appalachia. The hike is also part of the larger Buckeye Trail, the North Country Trail and the American Discovery Trail.

The Grandma Gatewood Trail is open daily from dawn until dusk, and summer and fall are the busiest times of the year. Visitors should come prepared for hiking in all weather and varied trail conditions. Along the way, hikers encounter a swirling pool of water called Devil's Bathtub, multiple waterfalls and an old fire tower on an 1,100-foot hill with stairs to views above the trees. Visitors can either hike the entire six miles or drive to each of these areas for shorter hikes to the main features.

Hocking Hills State Park is broken into seven scenic hiking areas with rock formations, waterfalls, recessed caves and unique flora and fauna: Old Man's Cave, Cedar Falls, Whispering Cave, Ash Cave, Conkle's Hollow, Rock House and Cantwell Cliffs. These areas were loved and explored by Gatewood for years. The park's main visitor center has information related to Gatewood.

Tessa Sweazy Webb Historical Marker

Hocking County, Logan, Ohio

(Ohio Literary Trail Map no. 59)

Location: Hocking County Historical Society Museum, southeast corner of East Hunter and North Culver Streets, just north of 64 North Culver Street, Logan, OH 43138

Latitude: 39.5407040, Longitude: -82.4027190

> MARKER TEXT
>
> *Born in 1886 on a farm near Logan, Tessa Sweazy Webb was a teacher at the Hocking County Children's Home where she began writing poetry. By 1924 she had become well-known across the state and nation for her published works. Under Webb's successful leadership and effort, the Ohio legislature passed a resolution in 1938 calling for an annual state observance of Ohio Poetry Day. Webb's work in Ohio was responsible for all fifty states observing Poetry Day. She received the Ohioana Award in 1942 for* Window by the Sea, *chosen as the best book of verse by an Ohio poet. In 1961, the Ohioana Library issued a citation citing her devotion to making Ohioans aware of Ohio Poetry Day. Webb died in 1979 in Logan at the age of ninety-three. Marker sponsors: Hocking County Historical Society, Logan-Holl Foundation, and The Ohio Historical Society.*

Burton Egbert Stevenson Historical Marker

Ross County, Chillicothe, Ohio

(Ohio Literary Trail Map no. 58)

Location: Chillicothe and Ross County Public Library, 140–146 South Paint Street, Chillicothe, OH 45601

Latitude: 39.3298630, Longitude: -82.9814450

> MARKER TEXT
>
> *Born in Chillicothe in 1872, Burton Stevenson's life was devoted to the written word as a prolific author and anthologist, and as a librarian. Following stints as a journalist while a student at Princeton University and then at newspapers in Chillicothe, Stevenson became the librarian of the city's public library in 1899. He held the post for fifty-eight years. Stevenson helped secure a Carnegie Library for Chillicothe, completed in 1906, and became prominent for his service during World War I. He*

Burton Stevenson at his desk. *Courtesy of Ohio History Connection (AL06667).*

founded a library at Camp Sherman, an army training camp north of the city, which became a model for others nationally.

Stevenson then went to Paris as the European director of the Library War Service. After the armistice in 1918, he established the American Library in Paris and directed it until 1920 and again from 1925 to 1930. In addition to accomplishments as a librarian, he wrote or compiled more than fifty books, including The Mystery of the Boule Cabinet *(1912), the* Home Book of Quotations *(1934), and many works for young people. Stevenson died in 1962. Stevenson Center, at Ohio University–Chillicothe, is named for him. Marker sponsors: Ohio Bicentennial Commission, The Longaberger Company, The Chillicothe and Ross County Public Library, and The Ohio Historical Society.*

Dard Hunter Historical Marker

Ross County, Chillicothe, Ohio

(Ohio Literary Trail Map no. 51)

Location: The Mountain House, 8 Highland Avenue, Chillicothe, OH 45601

Latitude: 39.3318740, Longitude: -82.9909960

MARKER TEXT

This classic Gothic Revival home built in the early 1850s was one of Ohio's early wineries with terraced hillside vineyards overlooking the city of Chillicothe. From 1919 until his death in 1966, it served as the home and working studio of noted American craftsman, artist, and historian Dard Hunter. A major artistic contributor to the Arts and Crafts Movement of the early twentieth century, Hunter gained international recognition when in 1916 he became the first individual in the history of printing to produce all aspects of a book by hand. Eight of the twenty books he wrote on the history of paper were printed at this site. Hunter is regarded as the world's leading authority on the history of paper and his artistic achievements have had an enduring impact on American Graphic Arts. Marker sponsors: Ohio Bicentennial Commission, Greater Cincinnati Foundation, and The Ohio Historical Society.

James Edwin Campbell Historical Marker

Meigs County, Pomeroy, Ohio

(Ohio Literary Trail Map no. 54)

Location: East Main Street at the park on the river side (just east of the intersection of OH 833 and OH 124), Pomeroy, OH 45769

Latitude: 39.0286980, Longitude: -82.0021030

MARKER TEXT

James Edwin Campbell was born on September 28, 1867, in the Kerr's Run area of Pomeroy to James and Letha Campbell. He graduated from Pomeroy High School with the class of 1884. After graduation, Campbell taught in various parts of Meigs County. Campbell achieved notoriety as an African American poet, editor, author of short stories, and educator. He began his writing in 1887 with the work Driftings and Gleanings. *During the 1880s and 1890s, he wrote regularly for daily newspapers in Chicago and was employed on the literary staff of the* Chicago Times-Herald. *His dialect poetry attracted widespread popularity and he published a collection of his best works,* Echoes from the Cabin and Elsewhere. *Campbell was installed as the first president of the West Virginia Colored Institute (West Virginia State University), serving in the position from 1891 to 1894. James Edwin Campbell died in Pomeroy on January 26, 1896. Marker sponsors: Meigs County Historical Society and The Ohio Historical Society.*

In the Area

Ambrose Bierce Historical Marker

Meigs County, Reedsville, Ohio
(Ohio Literary Trail Map no. 54)
Location: In front of Eastern Local High School, 38900 OH 7, Reedsville, OH
  45772
Latitude: 39.1224410, Longitude: -81.8831230

MARKER TEXT
An influential American journalist of the late nineteenth century, Ambrose Bierce (1842–c.1914) was born in Meigs County and reared in Kosciusko County, Indiana. He fought in the Union Army during the Civil War, a formative experience related in his short stories "Chickamauga" and "An Occurrence at Owl Creek Bridge." Moving to San Francisco in the years after the war, he began his career as a writer and newspaper columnist. His cynical wit and elaborate puns reached a wide audience during the last quarter of the nineteenth century through such papers as William Randolph Hearst's San Francisco Examiner. *Bierce's best-known book,* The Devil's Dictionary *(1911), is a lexicon of humorous definitions first published in his newspaper columns. In December 1913 or January 1914, Bierce vanished during travels in rebellion-torn Mexico. Marker sponsors: Ohio Bicentennial Commission, The Greater Cincinnati Foundation, and The Ohio Historical Society.*

Chapter 18

BELMONT AND JEFFERSON COUNTIES

William Dean Howells "Dean of American Letters" Historical Marker

Belmont County, Martins Ferry, Ohio
(Ohio Literary Trail Map no. 61)
Location: City Park, near 10 South Monument Avenue, Martins Ferry, OH
  43935
Latitude: 40.0967210, Longitude: -80.7244180

MARKER TEXT

Author, editor, and social critic William Dean Howells (1837–1920) was born in Martins Ferry, the son of an itinerant printer and publisher. Self-educated, Howells learned the printer's craft early and took up journalism, rising to city editor of the Ohio State Journal *(Columbus) in 1858. From 1871 to 1881, he was editor of the* Atlantic Monthly *magazine, a position of enormous influence in American literary tastes. Howells championed the work of Emily Dickenson, Paul Laurence Dunbar, and Stephen Crane, as well as several others. A prolific writer himself, he published over one hundred works. Howells is best known for his realistic fiction, including* A Modern Instance *(1882) and* The Rise of Silas Lapham *(1885). Many of his novels reflect his Ohio roots. Marker sponsors: Ohio Bicentennial Commission, The Longaberger Company, Greater Cincinnati Foundation, and The Ohio Historical Society.*

William Dean Howells.
Courtesy of Ohio History
Connection (AL02671).

James Arlington Wright Historical Marker

Belmont County, Martins Ferry, Ohio

(Ohio Literary Trail Map no. 61)

Location: City Park, near 10 South Monument Avenue, Martins Ferry, OH 43935

Latitude: 40.0967210, Longitude: -80.7244180

MARKER TEXT

James Arlington Wright was born in Martins Ferry on December 13, 1927. Wright's early life during the depression years was difficult, but he graduated as valedictorian from Martins Ferry High School in 1946. Wright later taught at the University of Minnesota and Hunter College (NY). A prolific writer, Wright published numerous books and volumes of his poetry, many of which included people and settings from Martins Ferry. In 1972, Wright was awarded a Pulitzer Prize in Literature. Wright died on March 25, 1980. Every April, Martins Ferry celebrates the James Wright Poetry Festival. Marker sponsors: Ohio Bicentennial Commission, The Longaberger Company, Greater Cincinnati Foundation, and The Ohio Historical Society.

In the Area

Andrew Carnegie/Carnegie Library of Steubenville Historical Marker

Jefferson County, Steubenville, Ohio
Location: Public Library of Steubenville and Jefferson County, 407 South Fourth
 Street, Steubenville, OH 43952
Latitude: 40.3551320, Longitude: -80.6180040

MARKER TEXT

Andrew Carnegie was born in Dunfermline, Scotland. He immigrated to Allegheny City, Pennsylvania with his family when he was thirteen. While operating the telegraphs for the Pennsylvania Railroad, Carnegie perceived the great need for steel in the railroad industry. With this insight, he founded the Carnegie Steel Corporation which operated for thirty-five years before he sold it to J.P. Morgan in 1901. Andrew Carnegie wrote the article, "Wealth" in 1889 in which he said that a responsible person of wealth should help his fellow man. Carnegie's philanthropy provided 2,509 libraries throughout the world. Carnegie was already familiar with the city when he wrote a letter to offer funds to build the Steubenville library on June 30, 1899.

As a young man, Carnegie was sent to a Steubenville telegraph office when a flood destroyed the wires between Steubenville and Wheeling. As part of his offer to build the library, Carnegie stipulated that the city's citizens would have to provide the site and money to maintain the library. The library was one of the first funded by Carnegie in Ohio and opened on March 12, 1902. Designed by the Pittsburgh architectural firm of Alden & Harlow, the Richardsonian Romanesque building shares its style with a smaller Oakmont, Pennsylvania library. Both libraries were designed using features of the 1888 Cambridge, Massachusetts city hall. The diagonal brick patterns on the ends of the structure are unique to this building. This library was added to the National Register of Historic Places in 1992. Marker sponsors: Public Library of Steubenville and Jefferson County Trust Fund and The Ohio Historical Society.

PART VII

Celebrating Today's Books, Writers and Readers

Chapter 19
LITERARY FESTIVALS AROUND OHIO

After traveling the state to visit historical sites, landmarks, museums and libraries featuring Ohio's literary greats, it's time to connect with today's literary talent. Ohio continues to inspire talented authors, poets, illustrators and more. There is no better place for readers to connect with current literary talent than the many annual book fairs and festivals around the state.

Many people recall the nostalgia of grade school years and warm memories when the gymnasium was converted to a giant bookstore for the annual book fair. Shelves of colorful paperbacks showcased titles from academic classics to trendy stories of the day, as well as a selection of fun accessories such as bookmarks and glitter pens. In addition to raising funds for the schools, these book fairs instilled a love of reading and shopping for books.

Book fairs in various forms have been around since Johannes Gutenberg's invention of the printing press. In 1454, Frankfurt, Germany, was the center of the publishing industry in the west and hosted the Frankfurt Book Fair. Today, it is the world's largest trade fair for books, connecting publishing companies, writers, illustrators, agents and other professionals, as well as readers.

The deep-rooted love of book fairs is alive for visitors of all ages at Ohio's book festivals. The Buckeye State offers a range of events that celebrate books, bring readers of all ages closer to the writers and illustrators who create them and create a marketplace for books. When readers meet the faces behind the creation of the stories and artwork, they are inspired to read more, and sometimes they even decide to write their own stories.

The Ohio Literary Trail selected one successful annual book fair or festival in each region of the state to showcase. While each event is unique, they all serve to introduce visitors to Ohio authors and topics related to Ohio. Because events adjust to changing circumstances, consult their websites in advance for the most current schedules.

NORTHWEST OHIO: CLAIRE'S DAY

Greater Toledo Area (Spring–May)
clairesday.org

Claire's Day Inc. was created in honor of the late Claire Lynsey Rubini. Her parents, Brad and Julie Rubini, wanted to honor the ten-year-old and her love of reading, storytelling, music, encouraging others to read and having fun with friends. They were inspired by former first lady Laura Bush's involvement in the Texas Book Festival, which features Texas-born authors and illustrators.

What began as a one-day free book festival in 2002 grew into a variety of literary experiences affecting more than fifteen thousand children annually. Claire's Day established a school outreach program, and visiting authors and illustrators are placed in Greater Toledo Area schools, where students hear their stories and inspirations.

After working in partnership, Read for Literacy and Claire's Day Inc. merged and formed a strategic alliance to continue providing programs in the Greater Toledo Area. Visit the website for dates and details at clairesday.org.

NORTHEAST OHIO: BUCKEYE BOOK FAIR

Wooster, Ohio (Fall–November)
buckeyebookfair.org

The Buckeye Book Fair is one of Ohio's premier book events, presenting a multi-day book festival held annually in Wooster at Fisher Auditorium. The book festival features more than one hundred Ohio authors and illustrators and thousands of attendees who shop for books and celebrate the joys of

Author Mark Dawidziak greets a fan. *Courtesy of Buckeye Book Fair.*

reading and writing. From writing activities to crafts and drawing workshops, there are literary activities for the entire family, including creative activities for children such as illustrator demonstrations.

A number of famous Ohio authors have participated in the Buckeye Book Fair over the years, including *Captain Underpants* creator Dav Pilkey, NASA astronaut Don Thomas, Olympic gold medalist Dominique Moceanu and Tuskegee Airman Dr. Harold Brown. Visit the website for current dates and details at buckeyebookfair.org.

Buckeye Book Fair was started by Wooster's newspaper, the *Daily Record*, as a fundraiser for literacy projects. To this day, Buckeye Book Fair donates more than $2,500 in books every year to Ohio schools and libraries. Buckeye Authors' Book Fair Committee Inc. was created as a nonprofit entity in 1987 and works exclusively with Ohio authors and illustrators to support literacy projects, including the annual book fair, author lectures and teacher and student workshops.

While you are in the area, historic downtown Wooster has many shops and eateries, a vineyard and a brewery, plus the Wayne County Historical Society and Museum. Numerous parks and nature centers offer sightseeing, as does Amish country, which is about twenty miles away and inspires authors of Amish stories.

Central Ohio: Ohioana Book Festival

Columbus, Ohio (Spring–April)
ohioana.org

The first Ohioana Book Festival was held at the Ohioana Library with ten authors in 2007, including fledgling Ohio author Anthony Doerr, who would later earn the Pulitzer Prize. Held each spring, the festival outgrew its original space and has relocated several times. In 2019, it was held at the Columbus Metropolitan Library's Main Library and featured more than 150 authors with more than 4,400 attendees throughout the day.

In addition to promoting and selling their books, Ohioana Book Festival authors participate in panels, workshops and readings, as well as outreach events around the state in advance of the festival. Readers of all ages connect with writers—from aspiring writers attending an "Introduction to Publishing" panel to teens meeting with YA authors and children listening to story time with popular picture book authors.

In 2020, when COVID-19 forced book events across the state to cancel, Ohioana took the unprecedented lead and hosted 140 authors and illustrators in a virtual festival with outreach events, moderated panels, seminars and book talks. Using a variety of online platforms and tools, the virtual Ohioana Book Festival produced more than thirty hours of festival programming. Visitors can revisit the recordings on the website to see the festival authors talk about their writing process, share their work and answer questions on everything a booklover or aspiring author could ever want to know.

To see future dates and schedules, visit ohioana.org.

Ohioana Book Festival at the Main Metropolitan Library in Columbus. *Photo by Mary Rathke.*

Southwest Ohio: Books by the Banks

Cincinnati, Ohio (Fall–October)
booksbythebanks.org

Books by the Banks Cincinnati Regional Book Festival is held annually in downtown Cincinnati and hosts visitors from Southwest Ohio and Northern Kentucky. The free daylong festival features national, regional and local authors and illustrators; book signings; panel discussions; and activities for the entire family to enjoy.

Visitors can hear their favorite authors talk about their work in fun, informative sessions and panel discussions, as well as meet authors in the Author Pavilion. Aspiring writers can hone their craft and connect with experts. Books by the Banks recognizes its best of the best with its annual Author Awards, which honor writing ability and thank the attending authors for contributing to the festival. Visit booksbythebanks.org for dates and details.

Southeast Ohio: Spring Literary Festival

Athens, Ohio (March or April)
ohio.edu/cas/English/news/events/spring-literary-festival

Since 1986, the Spring Literary Festival has featured some of the world's finest, most distinguished writers of poetry, fiction and nonfiction. The three-day festival is held on the campus of Ohio University and is organized by the English Department.

Unlike the larger festivals in Columbus, Wooster and Cincinnati, the Spring Literary Festival offers a more intimate format. The five visiting writers are present throughout the festival, lecturing and reading from their work, and books by the authors are available for purchase after each program. All readings and lectures are free and open to the public. For event dates and details, visit ohio.edu/cas/English/news/events/spring-literary-festival.

Appendix A
OHIO AUTHOR LISTING

In 2016, the Ohio Literary Map included the authors list, produced through the collaboration of the Ohioana Library Association, the Ohio Center for the Book at Cleveland Public Library and the State Library of Ohio. It was updated in 2020 by Ohioana Library Association for this publication.

It is not possible to name every notable writer, but this list is a representative sampling of those who have called Ohio home—whether born in Ohio (shown by an asterisk) or resided here three years or more. Other criteria for inclusion on this list include authors recognized as "classics," whose works continue to be read, studied and cited; authors who have won many major literary awards; and authors of very popular books. Regretfully, there may be omissions or errors.

Cartoons and Graphic Novels

Tom Batiuk*
Harmony Becker
Brian Michael Bendis
Jim Borgman
Milton Caniff*
R. Crumb
Justin Eisinger*
Billy Ireland*
Tony Isabella*
Jay B. Kalagayan*

R.F. Outcault*
Harvey Pekar*
P. Craig Russell
Joe Shuster
Jerry Siegel*
Jeff Smith
Brian K. Vaughn*
Bill Watterson
Tom Wilson Jr.*
Tom Wilson Sr.

Crime and Mystery Fiction

Delano Ames*
P.L. Gaus*
Elizabeth George*
Robert Greer
Karen Harper*
Chester Himes

Kristen Lepionka*
Olivia Matthews
Richard North Patterson
Les Roberts
Andrew Welsh-Huggins

Food Writing

Jeni Britton Bauer
Faith Durand
Eric LeMay
Michael Ruhlman*
Bev Shaffer

Del Sroufe
Marilou Suszko
Michael Symon*
Laura Taxel

History and Culture

Bob Batchelor*
Christine Brennan*
Douglas Brinkley
Mark Dawidziak
Martin Robison Delany
Michael Dirda*
David Giffels
Jean Gould*
Ann Hagedorn*
Wil Haygood*
Lafcadio Hearn
William Dean Howells*
Saeed Jones
Anne O'Hare McCormick
William Holmes McGuffey

Petroleum V. Nasby (David Ross Locke)
Susan Orlean*
Norman Vincent Peale*
Brad Ricca*
Julie Salamon*
Scott Russell Sanders
Arthur Schlesinger Jr.*
Ken Schneck
Connie Schultz*
Gloria Steinem*
Loung Ung
Carr Van Anda*
Elissa Washuta
Earl Wilson*
Victoria Woodhull*

Humor

Erma Bombeck*
Jake Falstaff* (Herman Fetzer)
Ian Frazier*
Mark O'Donnell*

P.J. O'Rourke*
Bentz Plagemann*
James Thurber*

Literary and General Fiction

Lee K. Abbott
Sherwood Anderson*
Ellis Avery
Michelle Baldini
Ambrose Bierce*
Kay Boyle
Louis Bromfield*
Dan Chaon
Charles Chestnutt*
Jennifer Chiaverini
Jennifer Cruise*
Anthony Doerr*
Allan W. Eckert
William Gass
Zane Grey*
O. Henry (William Sydney Porter)
John Jakes
Katrina Kittle

Lee Martin
Paula McLain
Toni Morrison*
Celeste Ng*
Robert Olmstead
Donald Ray Pollock*
Bonnie Proudfoot*
James Purdy*
Moriel Rothman-Zecher
Jack Warner Schaefer*
Curtis Sittenfeld*
Leah Stewart
Alison Stine*
Harriet Beecher Stowe
Thrity Umrigar
Edmund White*
Sarah Willis
Mark Winegardner*

Plays and Screenplays

W.R. Burnett*
Suzanne Clauser
Chris Columbus
Wes Craven*
Russell Crouse*
Michael Dougherty*
Joe Estevez*

Jim Jarmusch*
Adrienne Kennedy
Jerome Lawrence*
Chiquita Mullens Lee
Robert E. Lee*
Tad Mosel*
Eleanor Perry*

James Purdy*
Rod Serling
Steven Spielberg*

Donald Ogden Stewart*
Veena Sud

Poetry

Hanif Abdurraqib*
Kazim Ali
Maggie Anderson
Russell Atkins*
Ruth Awad
David Baker
George Bilgere
Imogene Bolls
Hale Chatfield
David Citino*
Hart Crane*
Wayne Dodd
Rita Dove*
Paul Laurence Dunbar*
Nikki Giovanni
Elton Glaser
Alvin Greenberg*
Richard Howard*
Andrew Hudgins

Langston Hughes
Marcus Jackson
Kenneth Koch*
Amit Majmudar
Howard McCord
Thylias Moss*
Aimee Nezhukumatathil
Mary Oliver*
Kenneth Patchen*
Stanley Plumly*
John Crowe Ransom
James Reiss
Elizabeth Spires*
David Wagoner*
Tessa Sweazy Webb*
Rachel Wiley*
Scott Woods*
James A. Wright*
David Young

Science Fiction and Fantasy

Matt Betts*
Gary Braunbeck*
Fredric Brown*
Lois McMaster Bujold*
Harlan Ellison*
Leanna Renee Hieber*
Ellen Klages*
Geoffrey Landis
Andre Norton*

Mike Resnick
Mary Doria Russell
John Scalzi
Lucy A. Snyder
Mary Turzillo
David Weber*
Kate Wilhelm*
Roger Zelazny*

Young Readers: Children and Middle Grades

Tony Abbott*
Arnold Adoff
Dan Andreasen
Natalie Babbitt*
Mildred Wirt Benson
Louise Borden*
Tim Bowers*
Michael Buckley*
Tamara Bundy
Mary Kay Carson
Andrea Cheng*
Sharon Creech*
Jeffrey Ebbeler
Denise Fleming*
Carole Gerber*
James Cross Giblin*
Margaret Peterson Haddix*
Virginia Hamilton*
Will Hillenbrand*
Anna Grossnickle Hines*
Michelle Houts*

Aiko Ikegami
Daniel Kirk
Lois Lenski*
J. Patrick Lewis
Loren Long*
Robert McCloskey*
Oge Mora*
Marilyn Nelson*
Shelley Pearsall*
Dav Pilkey*
Nancy Roe Pimm
Rafael Rosado
Michael J. Rosen*
Cynthia Rylant
Marcia Schonberg*
Tricia Springstubb
Carmella Van Vleet*
Jan Wahl*
Christina Wald*
Lindsay Ward
Jasmine Warga

Young Readers: Teens

Laura Bickle
Rae Carson
E.E. Charlton-Trujillo
Cinda Williams Chima*
Colleen Clayton*
Chris Crutcher*
Sharon M. Draper*
Angela Johnson
Lisa Klein
Mindy McGinnis
Robin McKinley*
Brandon Marie Miller

Edith Pattou
Amjed Qamar
Natalie Richards*
Debbie Rigaud
Kristen Simmons
Phil Stamper*
R.L. Stine*
Mildred D. Taylor
Stephanie S. Tolan*
Megan Whalen Turner
Jacqueline Woodson*

Appendix B

OHIOANA LIBRARY AWARD WINNERS

First given in 1942, the Ohioana Book Awards are the second-oldest, and among the most prestigious, state literary prizes in the nation. Nearly every major writer from Ohio in the past seventy-eight years has been honored, from James Thurber to Toni Morrison. The Ohioana Library presents juried awards in six categories: Fiction, Nonfiction, Juvenile Literature, Poetry, About Ohio/Ohioan and Middle Grade/Young Adult Literature. A special prize is given for emerging writers, the Walter Rumsey Marvin Grant. Fans select the Readers' Choice Book Award.

Fiction

NAME	YEAR	TITLE	COUNTY
Scibona, Salvatore	2020	*The Volunteer*	Cuyahoga
Rothman-Zecher, Moriel	2019	*Sadness Is a White Bird*	Greene
Ng, Celeste	2018	*Little Fires Everywhere*	Cuyahoga
Silver, Marisa	2017	*Little Nothing*	Cuyahoga
Russell, Mary Doria	2016	*Epitaph*	Cuyahoga
Doerr, Anthony	2015	*All the Light We Cannot See*	Cuyahoga
Hoffman, Beth	2014	*Looking for Me*	Hamilton

Name	Year	Title	County
Olmstead, Robert	2013	*The Coldest Night*	Delaware
McLain, Paula	2012	*The Paris Wife*	Cuyahoga
Doerr, Anthony	2011	*Memory Wall*	Cuyahoga
Chaon, Dan	2010	*Await Your Reply*	Cuyahoga
Kluge, P.F.	2009	*Gone Tomorrow*	Knox
Olmstead, Robert	2008	*Coal Black Horse*	Delaware
Avery, Ellis	2007	*The Teahouse Fire*	Franklin
Cunningham, Michael	2006	*Specimen Days*	Hamilton
Doerr, Anthony	2005	*About Grace*	Geauga
Morrison, Toni	2004	*Love*	Lorain
Doerr, Anthony	2003	*The Shell Collector*	Cuyahoga
Chaon, Dan	2002	*Among the Missing*	Cuyahoga
George, Elizabeth	2001	*In Pursuit of the Proper Sinner*	Trumbull
Paul, Terri	2000	*Glass Hearts*	Montgomery
Morrison, Toni	1999	*Paradise*	Lorain
Pierce, Constance	1998	*Hope Mills*	Butler
McGraw, Erin	1997	*Lies of the Saints*	Hamilton
Arthur, Elizabeth	1996	*Antarctic Navigation*	Butler
Gilfillan, Merrill, Jr.	1995	*Sworn Before Cranes*	Morrow
Frucht, Abby	1994	*Are You Mine?*	Lorain
Horowitz, Eve	1993	*Plain Jane*	Cuyahoga
Sloan, Kay	1992	*Worry Beads*	Hamilton
Zafris, Nancy	1991	*The People I Know*	Montgomery
Abbott, Lee K.	1990	*Dreams of Distant Lives*	Franklin
Boyle, Kay	1989	*Life Being the Best and Other Stories*	Hamilton
Robertson, Don	1988	*The Ideal, Genuine Man*	Cuyahoga
Dell, George	1987	*The Earth Abideth*	Butler

NAME	YEAR	TITLE	COUNTY
Nissenson, Hugh	1986	*The Tree of Life*	not an Ohioan
Pelletier, Nancy	1986	*The Rearrangement*	Washington
Skimin, Robert	1985	*Chikara!*	Medina
Hawley, Richard A.	1984	*The Headmaster's Papers*	Cuyahoga
Santmyer, Helen Hooven	1983	*...And Ladies of the Club*	Hamilton/ Greene
Berger, Thomas	1982	*Reinhart's Women*	Hamilton
Rosenblum, Helen Faye	1981	*Minerva's Turn*	Washington
Hill, Ruth Beebe	1980	*Hanta Yo: An American Saga*	Cuyahoga
Wagoner, David	1980	*The Hanging Garden*	Stark
Guild, Nicholas	1979	*The Summer Soldier*	Franklin
Jakes, John	1978	*The American Bicentennial Series* (Vols. 1–8)	Montgomery
Canzoneri, Robert	1977	*A Highly Ramified Tree*	Franklin
Harvey, Nancy Lenz	1976	*The Rose & the Thorn*	Hamilton
Morrison, Toni	1975	*Sula*	Lorain
n/a	1974	no award given	
Green, Hannah	1973	*The Dead of the House*	Hamilton
Bombeck, Erma	1972	*Just Wait Till You Have Children of Your Own*	Montgomery
n/a	1971	no award given	
Fish, Robert L.	1970	*The Xavier Affair*	Cuyahoga
McConkey, James	1969	*Crossroads*	Cuyahoga
Plagemann, Bentz	1968	*The Heart of Silence*	Clark
Eckert, Allan	1968	*The Frontiersmen*	Hamilton
Harrington, William	1967	*Yoshar the Soldier*	Washington
Knebel, Fletcher	1966	*The Night of Camp David*	Montgomery
Matthews, Jack	1965	*Bitter Knowledge*	Athens

NAME	YEAR	TITLE	COUNTY
Johnson, Josephine W.	1964	*The Dark Traveler*	Hamilton
Haydn, Hiram	1963	*The Hands of Esau*	Cuyahoga
DeCapite, Raymond	1962	*A Lost King*	Cuyahoga
Sinclair, Jo	1961	*Anna Teller*	Cuyahoga
Taylor, Peter	1960	*Happy Families Are All Alike*	Knox/ Franklin
Chamberlain, Anne	1959	*The Darkest Bough*	Washington
Locke, Charles O.	1958	*The Hell Bent Kid*	Seneca
Gold, Herbert	1957	*The Man Who Was Not With It*	Cuyahoga
Sinclair, Jo	1956	*The Changelings*	Cuyahoga
Young, Agatha	1955	*Clown of the Gods*	Cuyahoga
n/a	1954	no award given	
Ellis, William D.	1953	*The Bounty Lands*	Cuyahoga
Fridley, William	1952	*A Time to Go Home*	Allen
McConnaughey, Susanne	1952	*Point Venus*	Montgomery
Kelly, Amy	1951	*Eleanor of Aquitaine & the Four Kings*	Ottawa
Marshall, Robert Kossuth	1950	*Little Squire Jim*	Delaware
Deasy, Mary Margaret	1950	*Cannon Hill* (Honorable Mention)	Hamilton
Scott, Virgil	1949	*The Hickory Stick*	Franklin/ Cuyahoga
Young, Agatha	1949	*Light in the Sky* (Honorable Mention)	Cuyahoga
Freitag, George	1948	*The Lost Land*	Stark
Hannum, Alberta P.	1948	*Roseanna McCoy* (Honorable Mention)	Delaware
Diebold, Janet Hart	1947	*Mandrake Root*	Hamilton
Sinclair, Jo	1947	*Wasteland*	Cuyahoga

Name	Year	Title	County
Roberts, Dorothy James	1946	*A Durable Fire*	Washington
Southard, Ruth	1946	*No Sad Songs for Me* (Honorable Mention)	Lucas
Burnett, W.R.	1946	*Tomorrow's Another Day* (Honorable Mention)	Clark/ Franklin
Buckmaster, Henrietta	1945	*Deep River*	Cuyahoga
Carr, Robert Spencer	1945	*Bells of St. Ivan's* (2nd)	Franklin
DeCapite, Michael	1945	*No Bright Banner* (3rd)	Cuyahoga
McVicker, Daphne	1945	*The Queen Was in the Kitchen*	Franklin
Steward, Ann	1944	*Take Nothing for Your Journey*	Hamilton
Freeman, Martin Joseph	1943	*Bitter Honey*	Hardin
Williams, Ben Ames	1943	*Time of Peace* (Honorable Mention)	Jackson

Nonfiction

Name	Year	Title	County
Vanasco, Jeannie	2020	*Things We Didn't Talk About When I Was a Girl*	Erie
Giffels, David	2019	*Furnishing Eternity*	Summit
Stillman, Deanne	2018	*Blood Brothers*	Cuyhoga
Brinkley, Douglas	2017	*Rightful Heritage: Franklin D. Roosevelt and the Land of America*	Wood
Haygood, Wil	2016	*Showdown: Thurgood Marshall and the Supreme Court Nomination that Changed America*	Franklin

Name	Year	Title	County
Hagedorn, Ann	2015	*The Invisible Soldiers: How America Outsourced Our Security*	Montgomery
Ricca, Brad	2014	*Super Boys: The Amazing Adventures of Jerry Siegel and Joe Shuster—The Creators of Superman*	Cuyahoga
Zickefoose, Julie	2013	*The Bluebird Effect: Uncommon Bonds with Common Birds*	Washington
Orlean, Susan	2012	*Rin Tin Tin: The Life and the Legend*	Cuyahoga
Gup, Ted	2011	*A Secret Gift: How One Man's Kindness—and a Trove of Letters—Revealed the Hidden History of the Great Depression*	Stark
Collins, Gail	2010	*When Everything Changes: The Amazing Journey of American Women from 1960 to the Present*	Hamilton
Mansoor, Peter	2009	*Baghdad at Sunrise: A Brigade Commander's War*	Franklin
Hagedorn, Ann	2008	*Savage Peace: Hope and Fear in America 1919*	Montgomery/ Brown
Brinkley, Douglas	2007	*The Great Deluge: Hurricane Katrina, New Orleans, and the Mississippi Gulf Coast*	Wood
Maley, Saundra Rose	2006	*A Wild Perfection: The Selected Letters of James Wright*	not an Ohioan
Wright, Anne	2006	*A Wild Perfection: The Selected Letters of James Wright*	not an Ohioan
Zimmer, Paul	2005	*Trains in the Distance*	Stark

Name	Year	Title	County
Salamon, Julie	2005	*Rambam's Ladder: A Meditation on Generosity and Why It Is Necessary to Give*	Adams
Dirda, Michael	2004	*An Open Book: Coming of Age in the Heartland*	Lorain
Hagedorn, Ann	2004	*Beyond the River: The Untold Story of the Heroes of the Underground Railroad*	Montgomery
Salamon, Julie	2003	*Facing the Wind*	Adams
Fisher, Antwone Quentin	2002	*Finding Fish*	Cuyahoga
Mathias, Frank F.	2001	*The GI Generation: A Memoir*	Montgomery
Glenn, John	2000	*John Glenn: A Memoir*	Muskingum
Coan, Peter Morton	1999	*Ellis Island Interviews*	Cuyahoga
Haygood, Wil	1998	*The Haygoods of Columbus*	Franklin
Quammen, David	1997	*The Song of the Dodo*	Hamilton
Powell, Dawn	1996	*The Diaries of Dawn Powell, 1931–1965*	Morrow
Page, Tim	1996	*The Diaries of Dawn Powell, 1931–1965*	not an Ohioan
Frazier, Ian	1995	*Family*	Cuyahoga
Sanders, Scott Russell	1994	*Staying Put*	Portage
Marszalek, John	1993	*Sherman: A Soldier's Passion for Order*	not an Ohioan
Greene, Melissa Fay	1992	*Praying for Sheetrock*	Montgomery
Ward, Geoffrey C.	1991	*A First-Class Temperament: The Emergence of Franklin Roosevelt*	Licking
Wallace, David Rains	1990	*Bulow Hammock*	Franklin
Gilfillan, Merrill, Jr.	1989	*Magpie Rising*	Darke
Giovanni, Nikki	1988	*Sacred Cows…and Other Edibles*	Hamilton

Name	Year	Title	County
Cayton, Andrew R.L.	1987	*The Frontier Republic*	Hamilton/ Butler
Hutslar, Donald A.	1986	*The Architecture of Migration*	Franklin
Noble, Allen G.	1985	*Wood, Brick & Stone...*	Summit
Mott, Michael	1985	*The Seven Mountains of Thomas Merton*	Wood
Edmunds, R. David	1984	*The Shawnee Prophet*	not an Ohioan
Friedman, Lawrence	1983	*Gregarious Saints*	Wood
Trautman, Milton B.	1983	(for his body of work)	Franklin
Marcus, Jacob Rader	1982	*The American Jewish Woman*	Hamilton
Millett, Allan R.	1981	*Semper Fidelis: The History of the United States Marine Corps*	Franklin
Fensch, Thomas	1980	*Steinbeck and Covici: The Story of a Friendship*	Ashland
Unruh, John D., Jr.	1979	*The Plains Across*	Allen
Colinvaux, Paul	1978	*Why Big Fierce Animals Are Rare*	Franklin
Waldo, Terry	1977	*This Is Ragtime*	Franklin
Redinger, Ruby V.	1976	*George Eliot: The Emergent Self*	Cuyahoga
Mason, Ed	1976	*Signers of the Constitution*	Franklin
Mason, Ed	1976	*Signers of the Declaration of Independence*	Franklin
Ruksenas, Algis	1975	*Day of Shame*	Cuyahoga
Campbell, Michael	1975	*Water Well Technology*	Fairfield
Lehr, Jay H.	1975	*Water Well Technology*	Franklin
Young, Mahonri Sharp	1974	*The Eight*	Franklin

NAME	YEAR	TITLE	COUNTY
Smythe, Donald	1974	*Guerrilla Warrior: The Early Life of John J. Pershing*	Lorain
Hynek, J. Allen	1973	*The UFO Experience: A Scientific Inquiry*	Franklin
Cummings, Charles M.	1972	*Yankee Quaker Confederate General*	Franklin
Owens, Jesse	1971	*Blackthink*	Cuyahoga
Rousculp, Charles G.	1970	*Chalk Dust on My Shoulder*	Allen/ Franklin
Glueck, Nelson	1969	*The River Jordan*	Hamilton
n/a	1968	no award given	
Martin, John B.	1967	*Overtaken by Events*	Butler
Filler, Louis	1967	*The Unknown Edwin Markham*	Greene
Platt, Rutherford	1966	*The Great American Forest*	Franklin
Lee, Sherman E.	1965	*A History of Far Eastern Art*	Cuyahoga
Notestein, Lucy L.	1964	*Hill Towns of Italy*	Wayne
Smart, Charles Allen	1964	*Viva Juarez!*	Cuyahoga
Kendall, Paul Murray	1963	*The Yorkist Age*	Athens
Catton, Bruce	1962	*The Coming Fury*	Cuyahoga
Filler, Louis	1961	*The Crusade Against Slavery*	Greene
Jaffa, Harry V.	1960	*Crisis of the House Divided*	Franklin
Glueck, Nelson	1960	*Rivers in the Desert*	Hamilton
Carrighar, Sally	1959	*Moonlight at Midday*	Cuyahoga
Schlesinger, Arthur	1959	*Prelude to Independence: Newspaper War on Britain 1764–1776*	Greene/ Franklin
Schlesinger, Arthur, Jr.	1958	*The Crisis of the Old Order, 1919–1933*	Franklin
Kendall, Paul Murray	1958	*Warwick the Kingmaker*	Athens

NAME	YEAR	TITLE	COUNTY
Catton, Bruce	1957	*This Hallowed Ground*	Cuyahoga
Cady, John F.	1956	*Roots of French Imperialism in Eastern Asia*	Athens
Loesser, Arthur	1955	*Men, Women & Pianos*	Cuyahoga
Shinn, Roger L.	1954	*Christianity & the Problem of History*	Montgomery
Chalmers, Gordon K.	1953	*The Republic & the Person*	Knox
Swiggett, Howard	1953	*The Extraordinary Mr. Morris*	Brown
Radcliffe, Lynn James	1953	*Making Prayer Real*	Hamilton
Schwiebert, Ernest G.	1952	*Luther & His Times*	Henry
Catton, Bruce	1952	*Mr. Lincoln's Army*	Cuyahoga
n/a	1951	no award given	
Rodgers, Andrew Denny, III	1950	*Liberty Hyde Bailey*	Franklin
Nicholas, Edward	1950	*The Hours and the Ages: A Sequence of Americans*	Franklin
Peale, Norman Vincent	1950	*A Guide to Confident Living*	Greene
Hanford, James H.	1950	*John Milton, Englishman* (Honorable Mention)	Greene/ Cuyahoga
Kantonen, T.A.	1950	*Resurgence of the Gospel* (Honorable Mention)	Clark
Schlesinger, Arthur	1950	*Paths to the Present* (Honorable Mention)	Greene/ Franklin
Ostrom, John Ward	1949	*The Letters of Edgar Allan Poe*	Clark
Robinson, Howard	1949	*The British Post Office*	Cuyahoga
Luxon, Norval Neil	1949	*Niles' Weekly Register* (Honorable Mention)	Huron
Arbuthnot, May Hill	1949	*Children and Books*	Cuyahoga

Name	Year	Title	County
Joseph, Miriam, Sr.	1949	*Shakespeare's Use of the Arts of Language*	Putnam
Torrence, F. Ridgely	1949	*The Story of John Hope*	Greene
Wilson, John H.	1949	*The Court Wits of the Restoration* (Honorable Mention)	Clark/ Franklin
Livezey, William E.	1948	*Mahan on Sea Power* (Honorable Mention)	Belmont
Liebman, Joshua Loth	1947	*Peace of Mind*	Hamilton
Harrold, Charles F.	1947	*John Henry Newman* (Honorable Mention)	Belmont
Hibben, Frank C.	1947	*The Lost Americans* (Honorable Mention)	Cuyahoga
Morgan, Arthur Ernest	1947	*Nowhere Was Somewhere* (Honorable Mention)	Hamilton
Wittke, Carl F.	1946	*Against the Current: Life of Karl Heinzen*	Franklin
Schlesinger, Arthur, Jr.	1946	*The Age of Jackson*	Franklin
Adams, Philip R.	1946	*Auguste Rodin* (Honorable Mention)	Clark/ Hamilton
Schauffler, Robert H.	1946	*Florestan* (Honorable Mention)	Cuyahoga
Dulles, Foster R.	1945	*The Road to Tehran: The Story of Russia and America, 1781–1943*	Franklin
Henderson, Algo D.	1945	*Vitalizing Liberal Education*	Greene
Sockman, Ralph	1945	*Date with Destiny*	Knox
Seagrave, Gordon S.	1944	*Burma Surgeon*	Licking
Mills, Clarence A.	1943	*Climate Makes the Man*	Hamilton
Flory, William E.S.	1943	*Prisoners of War*	Stark
Taylor, Robert Emmett	1943	*No Royal Road*	Hamilton
Reston, James B.	1942	*Prelude to Victory*	Montgomery

NAME	YEAR	TITLE	COUNTY
Kiplinger, Willard M.	1942	*Washington Is Like That*	Logan
Havighurst, Walter	1942	*The Long Ships Passing*	Butler

Juvenile

NAME	YEAR	TITLE	COUNTY
Mora, Oge	2020	*Saturday*	Franklin
Woodson, Jaqueline	2019	*The Day You Begin*	Franklin
Derby, Sally	2018	*A New School Year*	Montgomery/ Hamilton
Payne, C.F.	2017	*Miss Mary Reporting*	Warren
Long, Loren	2016	*Little Tree*	Hamilton
Lewis, J. Patrick	2015	*Harlem Hellfighters*	Franklin
Cheng, Andrea	2014	*Etched in Clay: The Life of Dave, Enslaved Potter and Poet*	Hamilton
Bordon, Louise	2013	*His Name Was Raoul Wallenberg: Courage, Rescue and Mystery During World War II*	Hamilton
Carson, Rae	2012	*The Girl of Fire and Thorns*	Franklin
Cheng, Andrea	2012	*Where Do You Stay?*	Hamilton
Springstubb, Tricia	2011	*What Happened on Fox Street*	Cuyahoga
Rosen, Michael J.	2010	*Cuckoo's Haiku*	Franklin
Qamar, Amjed	2009	*Beneath My Mother's Feet*	Franklin
Haddix, Margaret Peterson	2008	*Uprising*	Fayette/ Delaware
Cheng, Andrea	2007	*The Lemon Sisters*	Hamilton
Draper, Sharon	2007	*Copper Sun*	Hamilton
Giblin, James Cross	2006	*Good Brother, Bad Brother: The Story of Edwin Booth and John Wilkes Booth*	Lake

Name	Year	Title	County
Borden, Louise	2005	*The Greatest Skating Race*	Hamilton
Pattou, Edith	2004	*East*	Franklin
Pearsall, Shelley	2003	*Trouble Don't Last*	Cuyahoga
Giblin, James Cross	2002	*The Amazing Life of Benjamin Franklin*	Cuyahoga
Durrant, Lynda	2001	*Betsy Zane: The Rose of Fort Henry*	Cuyahoga
Spires, Elizabeth	2000	*The Mouse of Amherst*	Fairfield
Durrant, Lynda	1999	*The Beaded Moccasins: The Story of Mary Campbell*	Cuyahoga
Rosen, Michael J.	1998	*The Heart Is Big Enough*	Franklin
Hamilton, Virginia	1997	*Her Stories: African American Folktales, Fairy Tales and True Tales*	Greene
Alder, Elizabeth	1996	*The King's Shadow*	Cuyahoga/Lake
Hickman, Janet	1995	*Jericho*	Franklin
Fleming, Denise	1994	*In the Small, Small Pond*	Lucas
Buchanan, Dawna Lisa	1993	*The Falcon's Wing*	Pike
Rylant, Cynthia	1992	*Appalachia: The Voices of Sleeping Birds*	Portage
Springstubb, Tricia	1991	*With a Name Like Lulu, Who Needs More Trouble?*	Cuyahoga
Rylant, Cynthia	1990	*But I'll Be Back Again*	Portage
Lewis, J. Patrick	1989	*The Tsar and the Amazing Cow*	Franklin
Curry, Jane Louise	1987	*The Lotus Cup*	Columbiana
Hamilton, Virginia	1984	(for her body of work)	Greene
Hoover, H.M.	1982	*Another Heaven, Another Earth*	Stark

NAME	YEAR	TITLE	COUNTY
Tolan, Stephanie S.	1981	*The Liberation of Tansy Warner*	Hamilton
Norton, Andre	1980	(for her body of work)	Cuyahoga
Curry, Jane Louise	1978	*Poor Tom's Ghost*	Columbiana
Turkle, Brinton	1977	*Island Time*	Stark
Turkle, Brinton	1977	*Deep in the Forest*	Stark
Stephens, Mary Jo	1976	*Witch of the Cumberlands*	Hamilton
O'Neill, Mary	1972	*Winds*	Cuyahoga
McKay, Robert	1971	*Dave's Song*	Franklin
Renick, Marion	1971	*Ohio*	Clark
Wahl, Jan	1970	*The Norman Rockwell Storybook*	Franklin/ Lucas
Hamilton, Virginia	1969	*The House of Dies Drear*	Greene
Friermood, Elisabeth H.	1968	*Focus the Bright Land*	Montgomery
Fife, Dale H.	1967	*Walk a Narrow Bridge*	Lucas
Eager, Edward M.	1963	*Seven-Day Magic*	Lucas
Vance, Marguerite	1962	(for her body of work)	Cuyahoga
De Borhegyi, Suzanne	1962	*Ships, Shoals & Amphoras*	Franklin
Schaefer, Jack W.	1961	*Old Ramon*	Cuyahoga
Kendall, Carol	1960	*The Gammage Cup*	Crawford
Eaton, Jeanette	1959	*America's Own Mark Twain*	Franklin
McCloskey, Robert	1958	*Time of Wonder*	Butler
Eager, Edward M.	1957	*Knight's Castle*	Lucas
Flora, James	1956	*The Fabulous Firework Family*	Logan
Scheele, William E.	1955	*Prehistoric Animals*	Cuyahoga
Anderson, Bertha C.	1954	*Tinker's Tim & the Witches*	Miami
Stewart, Anna Bird	1952	*Enter David Garrick*	Hamilton

NAME	YEAR	TITLE	COUNTY
Altick, Richard D.	1951	*The Scholar Adventurers*	Franklin
Havighurst, Marion	1950	*Song of the Pines*	Washington/ Butler
Wilson, Hazel	1950	*Island Summer*	Cuyahoga
Norton, Andre	1950	*Sword in Sheath*	Cuyahoga
McCloskey, Robert	1949	*Blueberries for Sal*	Butler
Lenski, Lois	1949	*Boom Town Boy*	Clark
Carrighar, Sally	1949	*One Day at Teton Marsh*	Cuyahoga
Harpster, Hilda	1949	*The Insect World*	Lucas
Treffinger, Carolyn	1948	*Li Lun, Lad of Courage*	Medina
Eaton, Jeanette	1948	*David Livingstone, Foe of Darkness*	Franklin
Evatt, Harriet	1947	*The Snow Owl's Secret*	Franklin
Bebenroth, Charlotta	1947	*Meriwether Lewis, Boy Explorer*	Cuyahoga
Thurber, James	1946	*The White Deer*	Franklin
Gall, Alice Crew	1946	*Splasher*	Morgan
Evatt, Harriet	1946	*Mystery of the Creaking Windmill*	Franklin
Crew, Fleming H.	1946	*Splasher*	Morgan
Fitch, Florence M.	1945	*One God: The Ways We Worship Him*	Lorain/ Hamilton
Thurber, James	1945	*The Great Quillow*	Franklin
Youmans, Eleanor	1945	*Mount Delightful*	Licking
Lenski, Lois	1944	*Bayou Suzette*	Clark
Stewart, Anna Bird	1943	*Bibi: The Baker's Horse*	Hamilton
Gilchrist, Marie Emilie	1943	*The Story of the Great Lakes*	Erie
Thomas, Eleanor	1943	*Mr. Totter and the Five Black Cats*	Franklin

Poetry

Name	Year	Title	County
Abdurraqib, Hanif	2020	*A Fortune for Your Disaster*	Franklin
Jackson, Marcus	2019	*Pardon My Heart*	Franklin
Awad, Ruth	2018	*Set to Music a Wildfire*	Franklin
Davis, Teri Ellen Cross	2017	*Haint*	Cuyahoga
Andrews, Nin	2016	*Why God Is a Woman*	Mahoning
Friebert, Stuart	2015	*Floating Heart*	Lorain
Ali, Kazim	2014	*Sky Ward*	Lorain
Collins, Martha	2013	*White Papers*	Lorain
Lucas, Dave	2012	*Weather: Poems*	Cuyahoga
David Young	2011	*Field of Light and Shadow: Selected and New Poems*	Lorain
Dove, Rita	2010	*Sonata Mulattica: Poems*	Summit
Greenway, William	2009	*Everywhere at Once*	Mahoning
Zimmer, Paul	2008	*Crossing to Sunlight Revisited: New and Selected Poems*	Stark
Weigl, Bruce	2007	*Declension in the Village of Chung Luong*	Lorain
Collins, Martha	2007	*Blue Front*	Lorain
Glaser, Elton	2006	*Here and Hereafter: Poems*	Summit
Fisher, Diane Gilliam	2005	*Kettle Bottom*	Franklin
Greenway, William	2004	*Ascending Order*	Mahoning
Spires, Elizabeth	2003	*Now the Green Blade Rises*	Fairfield
Roscoe, Jerry	2002	*Two Midwest Voices: Mirror Lake*	Franklin
DeMott, Robert	2002	*Two Midwest Voices: The Weather in Athens*	Athens
Belieu, Erin	2001	*One Above and One Below*	Athens

Name	Year	Title	County
Dove, Rita	2000	*On the Bus with Rosa Parks: Poems*	Summit
Baker, David	1999	*The Truth About Small Towns*	Licking
Citino, David	1998	*Broken Symmetry*	Franklin
Wagoner, David	1997	*Walt Whitman Bathing*	Stark
Matthias, John	1996	*Swimming at Midnight*	Franklin
Howard, Richard	1995	*Like Most Revelations*	Cuyahoga
Dove, Rita	1994	*Selected Poems*	Summit
Oliver, Mary	1993	*New and Selected Poems*	Cuyahoga
Moss, Thylias	1992	*Rainbow Remnants in Rock Bottom Ghetto Sky*	Cuyahoga
Citino, David	1991	*The House of Memory*	Cuyahoga/ Franklin
Dove, Rita	1990	*Grace Notes*	Summit
Shevin, David	1989	*The Discovery of Fire*	Seneca
Rosen, Michael J.	1985	*A Drink at the Mirage*	Franklin
Koch, Kenneth	1974	*Rose, Where Did You Get That Red?*	Hamilton
Oliver, Mary	1973	*The River Styx, Ohio and Other Poems*	Cuyahoga
Summers, Hollis	1968	*The Peddler & Other Domestic Matters*	Greene
Dell, George	1965	*Written on Quail & Hawthorn Pages*	Butler
Hodgson, Ralph	1961	*The Skylark & Other Poems*	Carroll
Wright, James	1960	*Saint Judas*	Belmont
Mears, Alice Monk	1946	*Brief Enterprise*	Cuyahoga
Robinson, Ted	1946	*Life, Love & the Weather* (Honorable Mention)	Cuyahoga

NAME	YEAR	TITLE	COUNTY
Ransom, John Crowe	1946	*Selected Poems* (Honorable Mention)	Knox
Patchen, Kenneth	1944	*Cloth of the Tempest*	Trumbull

About Ohio

NAME	YEAR	TITLE	COUNTY
McCullough, David	2020	*The Pioneers*	not an Ohioan
Haygood, Wil	2019	*Tigerland*	Butler
Alexander, Brian	2018	*Glass House*	Fairfield
Vance, J.D.	2017	*Hillbilly Elegy: A Memoir of a Family and Culture in Crisis*	Butler
McCullough, David	2016	*The Wright Brothers*	not an Ohioan
Diemer, Tom	2015	*James A. Rhodes: Ohio Colossus*	Franklin
Leonard, Lee	2015	*James A. Rhodes: Ohio Colossus*	Franklin
Goodwin, Doris Kearns	2014	*The Bully Pulpit: Theodore Roosevelt, William Howard Taft, and the Golden Age of Journalism*	not an Ohioan
Kiser, Joy	2013	*America's Other Audubon*	Summit
Millard, Candice	2012	*Destiny of the Republic: A Tale of Madness, Medicine and the Murder of a President*	Richland
Adoff, Arnold	2011	*Virginia Hamilton: Speeches, Essays, & Conversations*	Franklin
Cook, Kacy	2011	*Virginia Hamilton: Speeches, Essays, & Conversations*	Summit

Name	Year	Title	County
Meszaros, Gary	2010	*Wild Ohio: The Best of Our Natural Heritage*	Franklin
McCormac, James	2010	*Wild Ohio: The Best of Our Natural Heritage*	Cuyahoga
Giffels, David	2009	*All the Way Home: Building a Family in a Falling-Down House*	Summit
Haverstock, Mary Sayre	2008	*George Bellows: An Artist in Action*	Lorain
Hassler, David	2007	*Growing Season: The Life of a Migrant Community* (text)	Portage
Harwood, Gary	2007	*Growing Season: The Life of a Migrant Community* (photographer)	Portage
Rehak, Melanie	2006	*Girl Sleuth: Nancy Drew and the Women Who Created Her*	not an Ohioan
Souder, William	2005	*Under a Wild Sky: John James Audubon and the Making of* The Birds of America	not an Ohioan
Ritz, David	2004	*Faith in Time: The Life of Jimmy Scott*	Cuyahoga
Patton, Paul W. and Dorothy	2004	*Rix Mills Remembered: An Appalachian Boyhood*	Muskingum
Adams, Ian	2003	*Ohio: A Bicentennial Portrait*	Cuyahoga
Ostrander, Stephen	2003	*Ohio: A Bicentennial Portrait*	Franklin
Sallis, James	2002	*Chester Himes: A Life*	not an Ohioan
Sugden, John	2001	*Blue Jacket: Warrior of the Shawnees*	England
Mariani, Paul	2000	*The Broken Tower: The Life of Hart Crane*	not an Ohioan

NAME	YEAR	TITLE	COUNTY
Chernow, Ron	1999	*Titan: The Life of John D. Rockefeller, Sr.*	not an Ohioan
Langsam, Walter E.	1998	*Great Houses of the Queen City*	Hamilton
Olmstead, Earl P.	1998	*David Zeisberger*	Tuscarawas
Weston, Alice	1998	*Great Houses of the Queen City*	Hamilton
Foster, Emily	1997	*Ohio Frontier: An Anthology of Early Writings*	Franklin
Hoogenboom, Ari	1996	*Rutherford B. Hayes: Warrior and President*	not an Ohioan
Laycock, George	1995	*John A. Ruthven, in the Audubon Tradition*	Hamilton
Sacks, Howard L.	1994	*Way Up North in Dixie*	Knox
Sacks, Judith R.	1994	*Way Up North in Dixie*	Knox
Townsend, J. Benjamin	1993	*Charles Burchfield's Journals*	not an Ohioan
Knepper, George	1992	*Quilts in Community: Ohio's Traditions*	Summit
Clark, Ricky	1992	*Quilts in Community: Ohio's Traditions*	Lorain
Ronsheim, Ellice	1992	*Quilts in Community: Ohio's Traditions*	Wayne
Polster, Gary E.	1991	*Inside Looking Out*	Cuyahoga
Peterjohn, Bruce	1990	*The Birds of Ohio*	Franklin
Overmyer, Deborah	1989	*Bicentennial Guide to Greater Cincinnati*	Hamilton
Cincinnati Historical Society	1989	*Bicentennial Guide to Greater Cincinnati*	Hamilton
Giglierano, Geoffrey J.	1989	*Bicentennial Guide to Greater Cincinnati*	Hamilton

NAME	YEAR	TITLE	COUNTY
Blue, Frederick J.	1988	*Salmon P. Chase: A Life in Politics*	Mahoning
Tolzmann, Don Heinrich	1988	*The Cincinnati Germans After the Great War*	Hamilton
Matthews, Jack	1987	*Booking in the Heartland*	Athens
Koch, Freda Postle	1986	*Colonel Coggeshall: The Man Who Saved Lincoln*	Franklin
n/a	1985	no award given	
Joyce, Rosemary O.	1984	*A Woman's Place: The Life History of a Rural Ohio Grandmother*	Franklin
Westwater, James	1983	*Ohio*	Franklin
Rugoff, Milton	1982	*The Beechers*	not an Ohioan
Wallace, David Rains	1981	*Idle Weeds*	Franklin
Ohio Academy of Science	1980	*Ohio's Natural Heritage*	Franklin
Sanders, D.G.	1979	*The Brasspounder*	Perry
Peskin, Allan	1979	*Garfield*	Cuyahoga
Smith, Thomas H.	1978	*The Mapping of Ohio*	Athens
Warren, L.D.	1977	*The World & Warren's Cartoons*	Hamilton
Langsam, Walter C.	1977	*The World & Warren's Cartoons*	Hamilton
Laffoon, Polk, IV	1976	*Tornado*	Hamilton
Condon, George E.	1975	*Stars in the Water*	Cuyahoga
Anderson, Donald F.	1974	*William Howard Taft*	not an Ohioan
Young, Mahonri Sharp	1974	*The Paintings of George Bellows*	Franklin
Patterson, James T.	1973	*Mr. Republican: A Biography of Robert A. Taft*	not an Ohioan

Name	Year	Title	County
Davison, Kenneth E.	1973	*The Presidency of Rutherford B. Hayes*	Cuyahoga
Lynn, Kenneth S.	1972	*William Dean Howells: An American Life*	Cuyahoga
Taylor, John M.	1972	*Garfield of Ohio: The Available Man*	not an Ohioan
Manners, William	1971	*T R & Will*	Muskingum
Unterecker, John	1971	*Voyager: A Life of Hart Crane*	not an Ohioan
Frost, Lawrence A.	1970	*The Thomas A. Edison Album*	Lucas
Crunden, Robert M.	1970	*A Hero in Spite of Himself: Brand Whitlock*	not an Ohioan
Sawyer, Charles	1969	*Concerns of a Conservative Democrat*	Hamilton
O'Connor, Richard	1968	*Ambrose Bierce: A Biography*	not an Ohioan
n/a	1967	no award given	
Mason, Alpheus Thomas	1966	*William Howard Taft: Chief Justice*	not an Ohioan
Peltier, Leslie C.	1966	*Starlight Nights*	Allen
n/a	1965	no award given	
Morgan, H. Wayne	1964	*William McKinley & His America*	not an Ohioan
Sutton, Walter	1963	*The Western Book Trade*	Franklin
n/a	1962	no award given	
n/a	1961	no award given	
Leech, Margaret	1960	*In the Days of McKinley*	not an Ohioan
Sears, Alfred B.	1959	*Thomas Worthington: Father of Ohio Statehood*	not an Ohioan
n/a	1958	no award given	
Belden, Marva Robins	1957	*So Fell the Angels*	not an Ohioan

NAME	YEAR	TITLE	COUNTY
Belden, Thomas G.	1957	*So Fell the Angels*	not an Ohioan
n/a	1956	no award given	
n/a	1955	no award given	
Macartney, Clarence E.	1954	*Grant and His Generals*	Logan
Brown, Rollo W.	1954	*The Hills Are Strong*	Perry
n/a	1953	no award given	
Thomas, Norman	1952	*A Socialist's Faith*	Marion
Akeley, Mary L. Jobe	1951	*Congo Eden*	Harrison
n/a	1950	no award given	
n/a	1949	no award given	
Crile, Grace	1948	*George Crile: An Autobiography*	Cuyahoga
Crile, George, Sr.	1948	*George Crile: An Autobiography*	Cuyahoga
Cox, James M.	1947	*Journey through My Years: An Autobiography*	Butler
Havighurst, Walter	1947	*Land of Promise*	Butler
Raper, Howard Riley	1946	*Man Against Pain*	Ross
Hatcher, Harlan	1946	*Lake Erie* (Honorable Mention)	Lawrence
Hope, Bob	1945	*I Never Left Home*	Cuyahoga
Jordan, Philip Dillon	1944	*Ohio Comes of Age* (*History of the State of Ohio*, vol. 5)	Butler
Kelly, Fred Charters	1944	*The Wright Brothers*	Greene

Middle Grade and Young Adult Fiction

NAME	YEAR	TITLE	COUNTY
Warga, Jasmine	2020	*Other Words for Home*	Hamilton
Klages, Ellen	2019	*Out of Left Field*	Franklin

Bundy, Tamara	2018	*Walking with Miss Millie*	Hamilton
Derby, Sally	2017	*Jump Back, Paul*	Montgomery/ Hamilton
Pearsall, Shelley	2016	*The Seventh Most Important Thing*	Cuyahoga
Woodson, Jacqueline	2015	*Brown Girl Dreaming*	Franklin

Marvin Grant

NAME	YEAR	COUNTY
Curtinrich, Brendan	2020	Geauga
Grandouiller, David	2019	Greene/Franklin
Gellert, Christopher Alexander	2018	Franklin
Bethard, Ashley	2017	Montgomery
Goldbach, Elise	2016	Cuyahoga
Kaudo, Nigesti	2015	Franklin
Vanasco, Jeannie	2014	Erie
Matambo, Bernard Farai	2013	Lorain
Menkedick, Sarah	2012	Hamilton/Franklin
Walter, Laura Maylene	2011	Cuyahoga
Pribble, Daniel	2010	Butler
Cumming, Valerie	2009	Franklin
Kowalcyk, Nicholas	2008	Lorain
McClelland, Nicole	2007	Cuyahoga/Lake
McMullin, Jordan	2006	Trumbull
Kahn, Margot	2005	Hamilton/Cuyahoga
Goldhagen, Shari	2004	Hamilton
Hirt, Jen	2003	Cuyahoga
Avery, Ellis	2002	Franklin
Sickels, Amy	2001	Butler

Name	Year	County
Doerr, Anthony	2000	Geauga
Crane, Victoria	1999	Cuyahoga
Scibona, Salvatore	1998	Cuyahoga
Jackson, Jennifer	1996	Franklin
Young, Margaret	1994	Lorain
Upadhyay, Samrat	1992	Wayne
Tekulve, Susan	1990	Hamilton
Dick, David E.	1988	Lorain
Hinkle, Ann	1986	Butler
Hemley, Robin	1984	Athens
Adams, Elizabeth	1982	Cuyahoga

Readers' Choice Award

Name	Year	Title	County
Kaufman, Kenn	2020	*A Season on the Wind*	Ottawa
Wiley, Rachel	2019	*Nothing Is Okay*	Franklin
Bundy, Tamara	2018	*Walking with Miss Millie*	Hamilton
McDaniel, Tiffany	2017	*The Summer that Melted Everything*	Pickaway
Russell, Mary Dorira	2016	*Epitaph: A Novel of the OK Corral*	Cuyahoga

SOURCES

Sources appear here in order of their appearance in their respective chapters.

Chapter 1

Ohioana Library Association, Ohio Center for the Book at Cleveland Public Library and the State Library of Ohio. "Ohio Literary Map—Ohio Authors." Updated 2016 and 2020.

Wellborn, B.J. *Traveling Literary America: A Complete Guide to Literary Landmarks.* Canada, Jefferson Press, 2005.

World Population Review. "Ohio Population 2020." https://worldpopulationreview.com.

The University of Akron, Ray C. Bliss Institute of Applied Politics. "Basic Information on Ohio Politics #2: The 'Five Ohios': Ohio as a Microcosm of the Nation." September 8, 2020. www.uakron.edu.

Chapter 2

Verhoff, Andy. "Sixty Years of Marking Time." *Timeline* 35, no. 1 (January–March 2018): 50–54.

Weibel, Betty. "Ohio Literary Trail Launches This Summer." *Ohioana Quarterly* 63, no. 3 (Summer 2020): 16–18.

Chapter 3

Weaver, David. "Ohio Literary Trail: Celebrating Nancy Drew." *Ohioana Quarterly* 63, no. 3 (Summer 2020): 19.

Ohio History Connection/Remarkable Ohio. "Lucas County / 14-48 Toledo's First High School / Toledo-Lucas County Public Library." https://remarkableohio.org.

Ohio History Connection/Remarkable Ohio. "Lucas County / 2-48 House of Four Pillars." https://remarkableohio.org.

Chapter 4

Smith, Kristina. "Winesburg, Ohio at 100." *Ohio Magazine* (December 2019). https://www.ohiomagazine.com.

Ohio History Connection/Remarkable Ohio. "Sandusky County / 4-68 Sherwood Anderson." https://remarkableohio.org.

Ohio History Connection/Remarkable Ohio. "Erie County / 29-22 Sandusky Library / Erie County Jail." https://remarkableohio.org.

Chapter 5

Loar, Bryan. "The Mazza Museum, Ohio Literary Landmarks." *Ohioana Quarterly* 60, no. 3 (Summer 2017): 4–8.

Ohio History Connection/Remarkable Ohio. "Shelby County / 3-75 Lois Lenski." https://remarkableohio.org.

Ohio History Connection/Remarkable Ohio. "Van Wert County / 4-81 The Brumback Library." https://remarkableohio.org.

Ohio History Connection/Remarkable Ohio. "Paulding County / 2-63 Paulding County Carnegie Library." https://remarkableohio.org.

Chapter 6

Loar, Bryan. "Louis Bromfield and Malabar Farm." *Ohioana Quarterly* 59, no. 1 (Winter 2016): 4–7.

Ohio History Connection/Remarkable Ohio. "Richland County / 8-70 Louis Bromfield." https://remarkableohio.org.

American Library Association. "Oak Hill Dedicated 2000." www.ala.org.

Chapter 7

Peters, Morgan, and David Weaver. "Toni Morrison: A Tribute." *Ohioana Quarterly* 63, no. 1 (Winter 2020): 4–7.

Ohio History Connection/Remarkable Ohio. "Lorain County / 10-47 Helen Steiner Rice." https://remarkableohio.org.

Ohio History Connection/Remarkable Ohio. "Cuyahoga County / 47-18 Home of Superman." https://remarkableohio.org.

Ohio History Connection/Remarkable Ohio. "Cuyahoga County / 77-18 James Mercer Langston Hughes." https://remarkableohio.org.

Ohio History Connection/Remarkable Ohio. "Cuyahoga County / 12-18 The Oxcart Library." https://remarkableohio.org.

American Library Association. "Literary Landmark: Cleveland Heights— University Heights Public Library—Harvey Pekar." www.ala.org.

Chapter 8

Ohio History Connection/Remarkable Ohio. "Portage County / 5-67 Hart Crane, American Poet." https://remarkableohio.org.

Kessel, Laura. "Haines House Honored." *Alliance Review* (August 1, 2020): 1–3.

Chapter 9

Ohio History Connection/Remarkable Ohio. "Lake County / 15-43 Daniel Carter Beard." https://remarkableohio.org.

Ohio History Connection/Remarkable Ohio. "Geauga County / 12-28 The Second High School / The Burton Public Library." https://remarkableohio.org.

Ohio History Connection/Remarkable Ohio. "Trumbull County / 31-78 Bristol Public Library, 1912." https://remarkableohio.org.

American Library Association. "Literary Landmark: Earl Derr Biggers— Warren-Trumbull County Public Library." www.ala.org.

Chapter 10

Loar, Bryan. "Ohio Literary Landmarks: The Clocks of Columbus Set to Strike for Thurber." *Ohioana Quarterly* 62, no. 1 (Winter 2019): 4–6.

Ohio History Connection/Remarkable Ohio. "Franklin County / 78-25 James Thurber." https://remarkableohio.org.

Peters, Morgan. "Ohio's Literary Capitol: Celebrating Ninety Years with the Ohioana Library Association." *Ohioana Quarterly* 62, no. 3, (Summer 2019): 4–7.

Ohio History Connection/Remarkable Ohio. "Franklin County / 97-25 Columbus Main Library." https://remarkableohio.org.

Ohioana Quarterly 59, no. 3. "Billy Ireland Cartoon Library & Museum: Ohio Literary Landmarks" (Summer 2016): 4–8.

Loar, Bryan. "A Treasure House in Columbus: Theater History at the Lawrence and Lee: Ohio Literary Landmarks." *Ohioana Quarterly* 61, no. 3 (Summer 2018): 4–7.

Ohio History Connection/Remarkable Ohio. "Franklin County / 77-25 Wilbur H. Siebert Collection." https://remarkableohio.org.

Chapter 11

The Wagnalls Memorial. "A Historical Tour of the Wagnalls Memorial." wagnalls.org.

Chapter 12

Ohio History Connection/Remarkable Ohio. "Morrow County / 4-59 Dawn Powell." https://remarkableohio.org.

Ohio History Connection/Remarkable Ohio. "Knox County / 6-42 John Crowe Ransom & *The Kenyon Review*." https://remarkableohio.org.

Chapter 13

Ohio History Connection/Remarkable Ohio. "Hamilton County / 29-31 Harriet Beecher Stowe." https://remarkableohio.org.

Loar, Bryan. "Ohio Literary Landmarks: Mercantile Library." *Ohioana Quarterly* 60, no. 1 (Winter 2017): 4–9.

Ohio History Connection/Remarkable Ohio. "Hamilton County / 46-31 The Jacob Rader Marcus Center of the American Jewish Archives." https://remarkableohio.org.

Ohio History Connection/Remarkable Ohio. "Hamilton County / 51-31 Public Library of Cincinnati and Hamilton County." https://remarkableohio.org.

Ohio History Connection/Remarkable Ohio. "Butler County / 37-9 Clark Lane / Lane Public Library." https://remarkableohio.org.

Ohio History Connection/Remarkable Ohio. "Butler County / 12-9 William Dean Howells." https://remarkableohio.org.

Ohio History Connection/Remarkable Ohio. "Butler County / 39-9 Fannie Hurst—Author / Fannie Hurst—Humanitarian & Advocate." https://remarkableohio.org.

Ohio History Connection/Remarkable Ohio. "Butler County / 14-9 William Holmes McGuffey House." https://remarkableohio.org.

Ohio History Connection/Remarkable Ohio. "Butler County / 38-9 'The Poet's Shack'/ Percy MacKaye." https://remarkableohio.org.

Chapter 14

Loar, Bryan. "The Dunbar House: Ohio Literary Landmarks." *Ohioana Quarterly* 61, no. 1 (Winter 2018): 4–7.

Ohio History Connection/Remarkable Ohio. "Montgomery County / 8-57 Paul Laurence Dunbar." https://remarkableohio.org.

Ohio History Connection/Remarkable Ohio. "Montgomery County / 16-57 Natalie Clifford Barney." https://remarkableohio.org.

Ohio History Connection/Remarkable Ohio. "Greene County / 17-29 Hallie Quinn Brown." https://remarkableohio.org.

Ohio History Connection/Remarkable Ohio. "Greene County / 19-29 Helen Hooven Santmyer." https://remarkableohio.org.

Ohio History Connection/Remarkable Ohio. "Greene County / 29-29 Virginia Hamilton." https://remarkableohio.org.

Chapter 15

Ohio History Connection/Remarkable Ohio. "Brown County / 5-8 Historic Decatur." https://remarkableohio.org.

Ohio History Connection/Remarkable Ohio. "Highland County/ 4-36 Milton Caniff." https://remarkableohio.org.

Ohio History Connection/Remarkable Ohio. "Clinton County / 9-14 Wilmington Library." https://remarkableohio.org.

Chapter 16

Carpenter, Robert. "Zane Grey National Road Museum." 2000. ohiotraveler.com.

Ohio History Connection/Remarkable Ohio. "Muskingum County / 13-60 Zane Grey 'Father of the Western Novel.'" https://remarkableohio.org.

Ohio Department of Natural Resources. "New Storybook Trails Open at Four Ohio State Parks, Trails Promote Fun and Reading for Kids of All Ages." News release, June 11, 2020. https://ohiodnr.gov.

Ohio History Connection/Remarkable Ohio. "Morgan County / 12-58 Frances Dana Gage / Mount Airy Mansion." https://remarkableohio.org.

Ohio History Connection/Remarkable Ohio. "Athens County / 5-5 Western Library Association, 1804—The Coonskin Library." https://remarkableohio.org.

Ohio History Connection/Remarkable Ohio. "Washington County / 9-84 Putnam Family Library/Belpre Farmers' Library." https://remarkableohio.org.

Chapter 17

Seelye, Katharine Q. "Overlooked No More: Emma Gatewood, First Woman to Conquer the Appalachian Trail Alone." *New York Times*, July 23, 2018, 16.

Sell, Jill. "Appalachia: Four Great Hikes." *Ohio Magazine* (July 2018). https://www.ohiomagazine.com.

Ohio History Connection/Remarkable Ohio. "Hocking County / 6-37 Tessa Sweazy Webb—Founder of Ohio Poetry Day." https://remarkableohio.org.

Ohio History Connection/Remarkable Ohio. "Ross County / 9-71 Burton Egbert Stevenson." https://remarkableohio.org.

Ohio History Connection/Remarkable Ohio. "Ross County / 13-71 Dard Hunter." https://remarkableohio.org.

Ohio History Connection/Remarkable Ohio. "Meigs County / 19-53 James Edwin Campbell." https://remarkableohio.org.

Ohio History Connection/Remarkable Ohio. "Meigs County / 15-53 Birthplace of Ambrose Bierce." https://remarkableohio.org.

Chapter 18

Ohio History Connection/Remarkable Ohio. "Belmont County / 12-7 William Dean Howells, 'The Dean of American Letters' / Poet James Arlington Wright." https://remarkableohio.org.

Ohio History Connection/Remarkable Ohio. "Jefferson County / 10-41 Andrew Carnegie (1835–1919) / Carnegie Library of Steubenville." https://remarkableohio.org.